The Illustrated ROCK QUIZ

Rob Burt

Exeter Books
NEW YORK

Editor : **Felicity Smart**
Designer : **Rob Burt**

First published in the United States of America in 1979
by Exeter Books
Distributed by Bookthrift, Inc.
New York, New York

Printed in Great Britain

ISBN : 0-89673-020-4

Library of Congress Catalog Card Number : 79-52187

This book may not be sold outside of the United States
of America or its territories.

Illustrations
Title page : Still from the
film *Some People*
Introduction : **Diana Ross**
Quiz Guide : **The Beatles**

Quiz Guide...

Superstars:

Starfiles:

Check your answers by looking up the quiz number in the answer section

About This Book...

When the history of the twentieth century comes to be written, rock music - with its amazingly varied sub-culture - will undoubtedly take its place as a major force among the arts . . . with **Presley** rubbing shoulders with **Picasso, Hendrix** with **Hemingway, The Stones** with **Stravinsky,** and **Charles Westover** with - *Charles who*? Who *is* **Charles Westover**? Just one of the many key questions I've posed in this book.

In writing *The Illustrated Rock Quiz,* I've aimed to include a wide range of questions vital to an in-depth knowledge of rock and popular music - and which also present the story of popular music in an entertaining and informative way. It not only features the up-front performers - the big names of the business - but also covers the behind-the-scenes people who help create the hits.

Packed with photos, some of them rarely seen now, *Rock Quiz* will revive memories and show the unique styles of the all-time greats. Each of the ninety-six quizzes scores points to tell you how expert you are, and the answers given at the back of the book could be the ones you always wanted to know about rock music.

I've tried to transmit the fun and the thrill of the pop scene in these pages, while being only too well aware of the incredibly hard work that goes into any chart-topping success. I've also tried to collect together much of the information which until now was only to be found scattered in music magazines and on album sleeves, so that *The Illustrated Rock Quiz* will be a useful source of reference.

Spanning more than twenty years of golden hits, including all the great trends and trendsetters from **Presley** and **Haley** to **Clapton** and **Costello,** this book will, I sincerely hope, bring you as much pleasure as compiling and designing it gave me.

Rob Burt

Right: Olivia Newton-John (see 1. H)

1 Rock All-Sorts

(General; worth 2 points each)

A) Name the individuals who form **Abba.**

B) Who is known as 'the man with the twangy guitar'?

C) What phrase is used to describe **Phil Spector's** production technique?

D) Name the four **Gibb** brothers.

E) What have **Dobie Gray, Ramsey Lewis** and **Bryan Ferry** in common?

F) Under what name did **Simon and Garfunkel** have their *Hey Schoolgirl* hit?

G) Name **Elvis Costello's** first single.

H) Where was **Olivia Newton-John** born?

I) What was the name of the famous Liverpool cellar club, home of the sixties' Mersey sound?

J) What is the **Osmond's** religion?

K) Which group formed **Apple** records?

L) Name the individual **Mamas and Papas.**

M) Which UK football club is **Elton John** connected with?

N) Where did **The Beach Boys** hail from?

O) Who was **The Ramones'** *Punk Rocker*?

P) Where were **Boney M** asked not to perform their *Rasputin* hit?

Q) What is the twelfth song on **Randy Newman's** *12 Songs* album?

R) Who wore the Union Jack on **The Who's** *My Generation* album sleeve?

S) Name the four **Pointer Sisters.**

T) Who is **Debbie Boone's** famous dad?

U) In what film did **Connie Francis** make her acting debut?

V) Kate, Alex and Livingston have a famous sister-in-law. Who is she?

W) Name the site of the Woodstock rock festival.

X) What term is used to describe fifties' street corner harmony groups?

Y) Who was famous for his kiss-curl?

Z) When was (full date) **The Beatles'** *Sergeant Pepper's Lonely Hearts Club Band* album released?

2 Hail, Hail, Rock 'n' Roll

(Specialist; worth 3 points each)

A) Who introduced the duck-walk ?

B) In '56 what did **Carl Perkins** ask us not to step on ?

C) Who claimed to have invented the term **Rock 'n' Roll** ?

D) What was **Buddy Holly's** full name ?

E) *The Stroll* and *Little Darlin'* were both big hits for a group of singers. What were they called ?

F) In which film was **Bill Haley's** *Rock Around the Clock* first heard ?

G) **Eddie Cochran** recorded the same song twice but changed its title. Name both titles.

H) Name **Duane Eddy's** backing group.

I) Name the individual **Teddy Bears.**

J) What was **J. P. Richardson** better known as ?

K) What is **Bill Haley's** full name ?

L) Name **Chuck Berry's** first million-selling single.

M) Where did **Little Richard** hail from and what is his full name ?

N) What label did **The Platters** originally record on ?

O) **Mae Boren Axton** who wrote *Heartbreak Hotel* for **Presley** also penned a hit for **Buchanan and Goodman.** What was its title ?

P) What instrument was **Bill Doggett** famous for playing ?

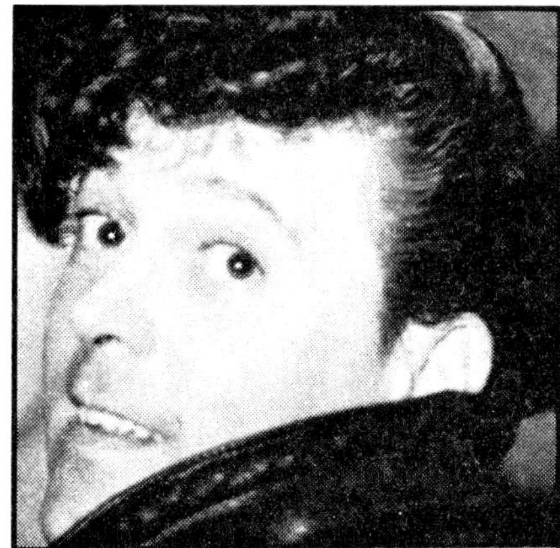

Q) Name **Gene Vincent's** backing group .

R) In **Chuck Berry's** *School Days* what two subjects is he "studyin' hard, hopin' to pass" ?

S) Who is known as **The Killer** ?

T) Where were **Danny and The Juniors** in '57 ?

U) What are the Christian names of **The Everly Brothers** ?

V) Released in '48, when did **Fats Domino's** *Fat Man* certify gold ?

W) Who is **Robert Byrd** better known as ?

X) In what '57 **Rock 'n' Roll** movie did **Jerry Lee Lewis** perform *Great Balls of Fire* ?

Y) He starred opposite **James Dean** in *Rebel Without A Cause* and won chart honours with *Start Movin'* (*in my direction*). What is his name ?

Z) Who were the three stars who lost their lives after a tragic plane crash near Mason City, Iowa, and on what date did it happen ?

Below: Bill Haley & The Comets (*see* 2. F & K)

3 Superstars/Elvis Presley

(Specialist; worth 3 points each)

Elvis Presley outsold, outfilmed, outrocked and outraged more people than any other figure in the world of rock. Truly rock's first great innovator, he was the undisputed King of Rock 'n' Roll.

A) Where and when was **Elvis** born ?
B) What was his full name ?
C) How old was he when the **Presley** family moved to Memphis ?

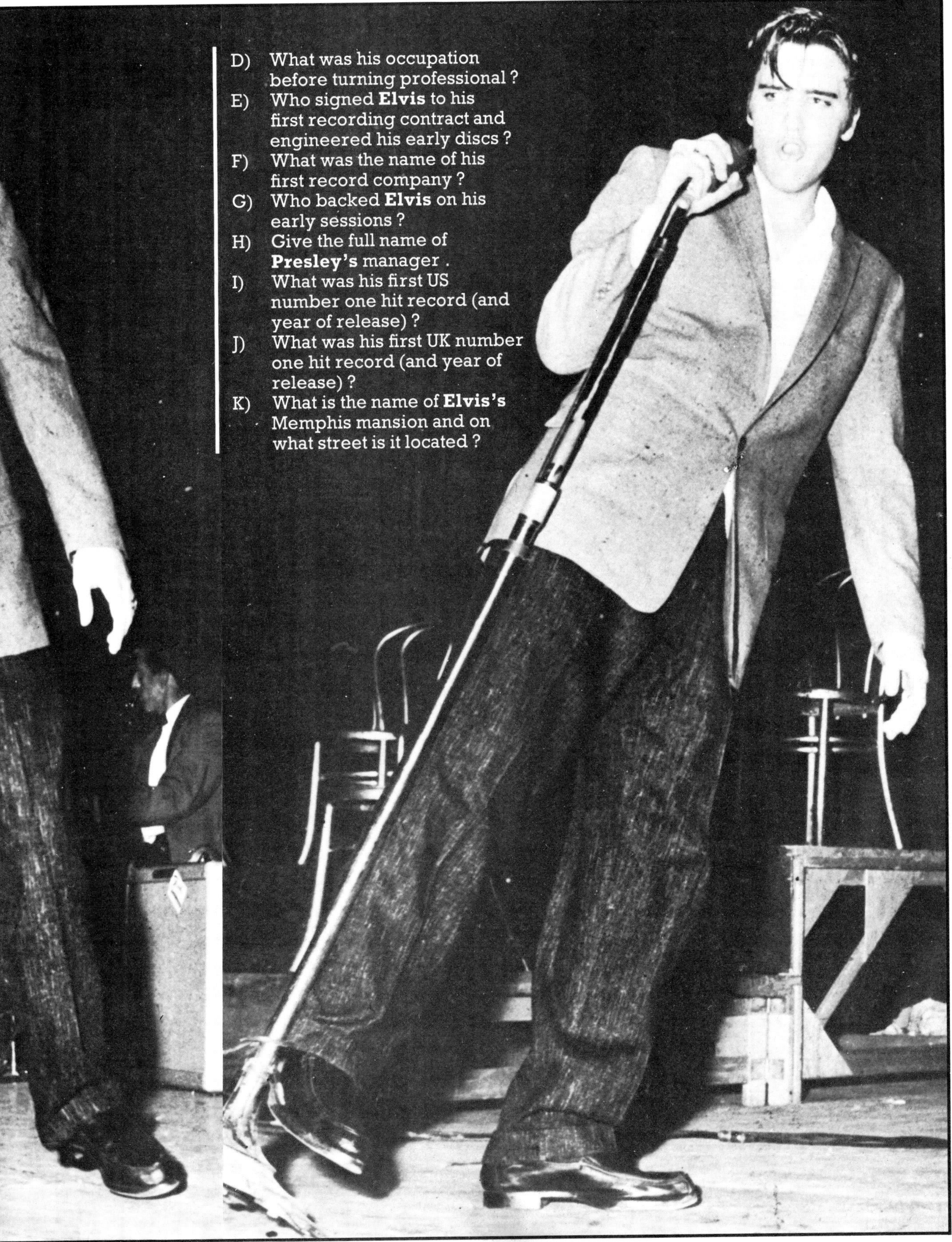

D) What was his occupation before turning professional ?
E) Who signed **Elvis** to his first recording contract and engineered his early discs ?
F) What was the name of his first record company ?
G) Who backed **Elvis** on his early sessions ?
H) Give the full name of **Presley's** manager .
I) What was his first US number one hit record (and year of release) ?
J) What was his first UK number one hit record (and year of release) ?
K) What is the name of **Elvis's** Memphis mansion and on what street is it located ?

L) What was the full date of his introduction into the army and what year was he demobbed ?

M) Did **Elvis** ever visit the UK ? If so, where and why ?

N) What was his first joint US and UK number one hit record after his army service ?

O) Who, and when, did **Elvis** marry ?

P) What is the name of his daughter ?

Q) What is the full date of **Elvis Presley's** death ?

4 Presley films

(Specialist; worth 3 points each)

A) Who produced his first movie and what was its title ?

B) How many of **Elvis's** films were produced by **Hal Wallis** ?

C) Who directed his 6th film and what was its title ?

D) Name the films in which **Elvis** played

1. A half-breed Kiowa Indian
2. A boxer
3. A doctor
4. A photographer
5. A pilot
6. A manager of a travelling show
7. A navy diver
8. A GI

5 Starfile/Bobby Darin

(Specialist; worth 3 points each)

A) Who co-wrote his first song (released in '56 on **Decca**), *My First Love* ?

B) What is the title of the big hit which launched his chart-topping career ?

C) Name his joint US and UK number one hit single, and the title of the album it was culled from.

D) In 1960 he married teen actress **Alexandra Zuck.** By what name is **Miss Zuck** better known ?

E) Name two out of the three movies he appeared in opposite his wife.

F) What instrumental film theme was released as a single and credited to **The Bobby Darin Orchestra** ?

G) Who was his songwriting partner on hot-rod songs (recorded by groups like **The Surfaris** and **The Rip Chords**) ?

H) In what movie did he co-star with **Sidney Poitier** ?

I) What was the title of his last big international hit single ?

J) When was **Bobby's** untimely death ?

Picture Quiz 1

(Specialist; worth 3 points each)

A) Who are these hit songwriters ?

B) The pianist is one half of a famous duo. Name the duo, the other half, and say how they are related to each other.

C) What is the full title of the **Klaatu** song they successfully covered ?

D) Where are they pictured here ?

Below: Eddie Cochran ***(see* 6. P)**

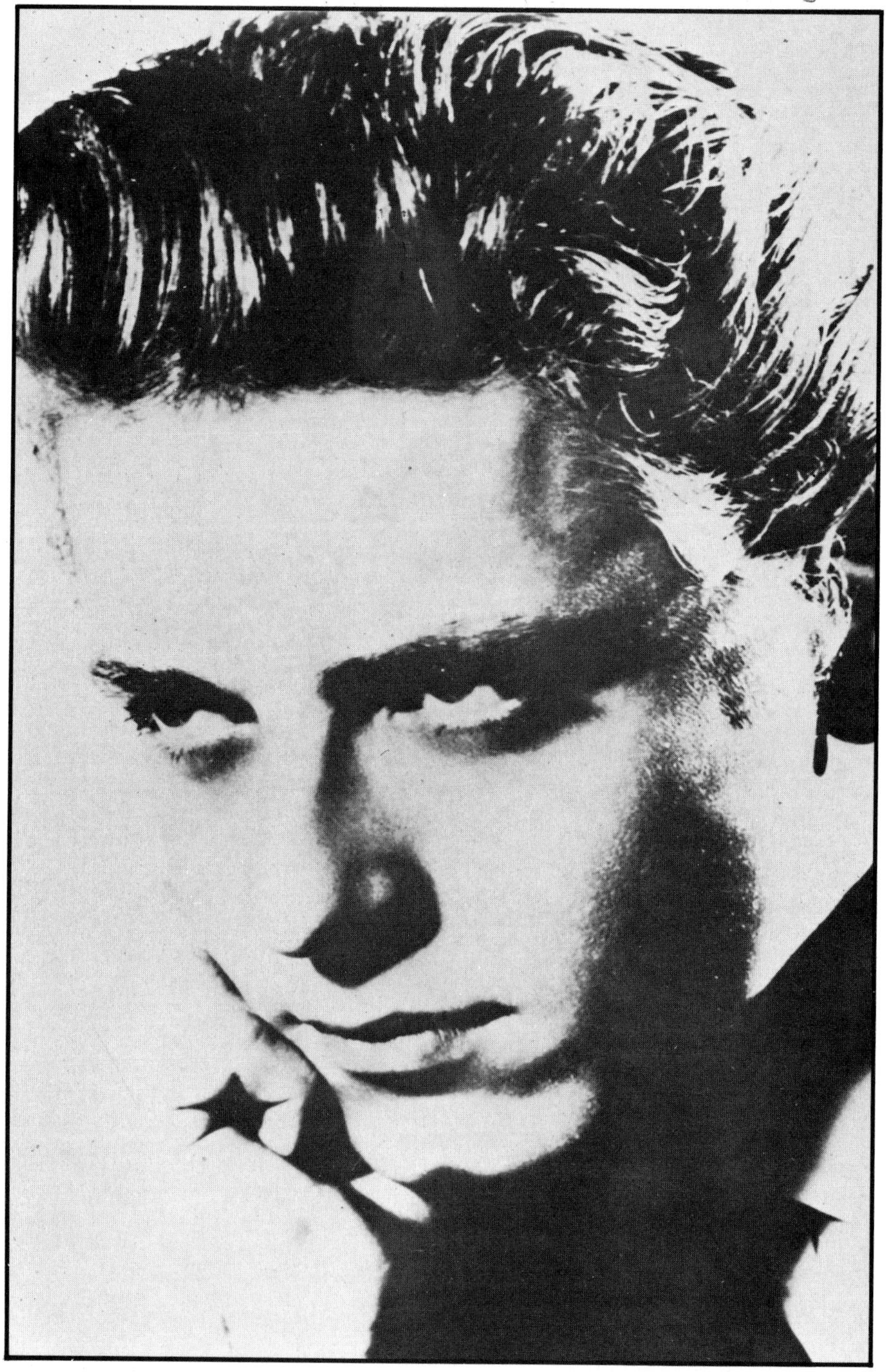

6 Hail, Hail, Rock 'n' Roll

(Specialist; worth 3 points each)

A) Who is known as **The Big O**?

B) On which **Platters'** single did **Zola Reed** make her debut?

C) Name **Frankie Lyman's Teenagers.**

D) **Johnny Burnette** also recorded as one half of **The Burnette Brothers.** What is his brother's name?

E) Where did *Ko Ko Mo* have her dimples?

F) What was the name of **Alan Freed's** first Rock 'n' Roll radio show?

G) Who were the four **Sun** recording artistes who gathered around a piano and cut *Peace in the Valley* in the summer of '56?

H) Which song did **Chuck**

Berry perform in the film *Jazz on a Summer's Day*?

I) Where was the original **Dot** label based?

J) Who scored with *Party Doll* in '57?

K) In *Trouble*, what was **Elvis's** dad?

L) When was **Dick Clark's** *American Bandstand* TV show first broadcast, and on what station?

M) By what name is **Elias McDaniel** better known?

N) In which Western TV series did **Duane Eddy** make a guest appearance?

O) What is **Fabian's** full name?

P) On what date was **Eddie Cochran** killed in an auto accident?

Q) In which '56 movie did **Gene Vincent** and **The Bluecaps** perform *Be-Bop-A-Lula*?

R) Name **Buddy Holly's** backing group.

S) What is **Fats Domino's** full name?

T) Who did **The Saddlemen**

Below: **Johnny Burnette** (*see* 6. D)

become ?

U) What is known as the 'tradesman's knock'?

V) Who scored with the '59 instrumental hit, *Red River Rock* ?

W) Two members of **The Rhythm Orchids** left to pursue successful solo careers. Who were they ?

X) Name the American folk song on which **Lloyd Price** based his *Stagger Lee.*

Y) **Little Richard** released four songs under his group's name. Give the group's name and the titles of the songs .

Z) By what name is **Jack Scufone** better known ?

7 Rock All-Sorts

(General; worth 2 points each)

A) Name the trio of *Schmilsson* albums by **Harry Nilsson.**

B) By what name is **John Henry Deutschendorf** better known ?

C) Where did the **A & M/Sex Pistols** signing take place ?

D) Who penned *Something In The Way She Moves* ?

E) **Edward Byrnes** and **Connie Stevens** scored with a song that cashed in on the popularity of the former's TV role in *77 Sunset Strip*. What was its title, and in what TV series was **Connie Stevens** regularly featured ?

F) Who shared *The Graduate* soundtrack with **Simon and Garfunkel** ?

G) What was the original title of **The Monkees'** *Alternate Title* ?

H) From what album was **Ace's** big hit *How Long* culled ?

I) **Don McLean's** song *Vincent* was based on which famous artist ?

J) Under what name was **Slade** originally known ?

K) Who in '59 held the *Deck of Cards* ?

L) What was **Amen Corner's** follow-up to their *Gin House* hit ?

M) Who cut the original version of *Louie Louie* ?

N) What is the title of **Captain Beefheart's** first album ?

O) Who sings with **The Attractions** ?

P) What label did **Ronny and The Daytonas** record on ?

Q) Which ex-member of **The Zombies** recorded under the name **Neil McArthur** ?

R) By what name is Reggae's **James Chambers** better known ?

S) What was **Love Sculpture's** big instrumental hit, and who featured on lead guitar ?

T) Who is **Mentor Williams'** singer/songwriter brother ?

U) Producer **Ted Templeman** was once a member of a hit recording group. What was its name ?

V) Who scored in '78 with a disco version of **Jim Webb's** *MacArthur Park* ?

W) What is **Little Eva's** full name ?

X) With whom did **Bobbie Gentry** duet on her *All I Have to do is Dream* hit ?

Y) Name two songs with *Sun* in their titles that were both reported to have been composed on the night of Friday, November 22 '63 following **President J. F. Kennedy's** assassination.

Z) Who has managed (full name) both **Jimi Hendrix** and **Slade** ?

8 Who are they ?

(General; worth 2 points each)

Stage names have always been a stock-in-trade with movie personalities, but many rock stars also choose to change their names for a more glamorous or memorable one.

By what names are the following better known ?

A) Charles Westover
B) Constance Franconero
C) Vince Furnier
D) Harry Webb
E) Mary O'Brien
F) Lugee Salo
G) Steven Georgiou
H) Benjamin Earl Nelson
I) Sandra Goodrich
J) Walden Robert Cassatto
K) Reg Dwight
L) Arnold George Dorsey
M) Charles Eugene Boone
N) Roberta Streeter
O) David Jones
P) Arthur Gelie
Q) John Lydon
R) Geraldine Ann Pasquale
S) Harold Jenkins
T) Richard Valenzuela
U) Marie McDonald McLaughlin Lawrie
V) Benjamin Franklin Peay
W) Frederick A. Picariello
X) John Deighton
Y) Robert Louis Ridarelli
Z) Ernest Evans

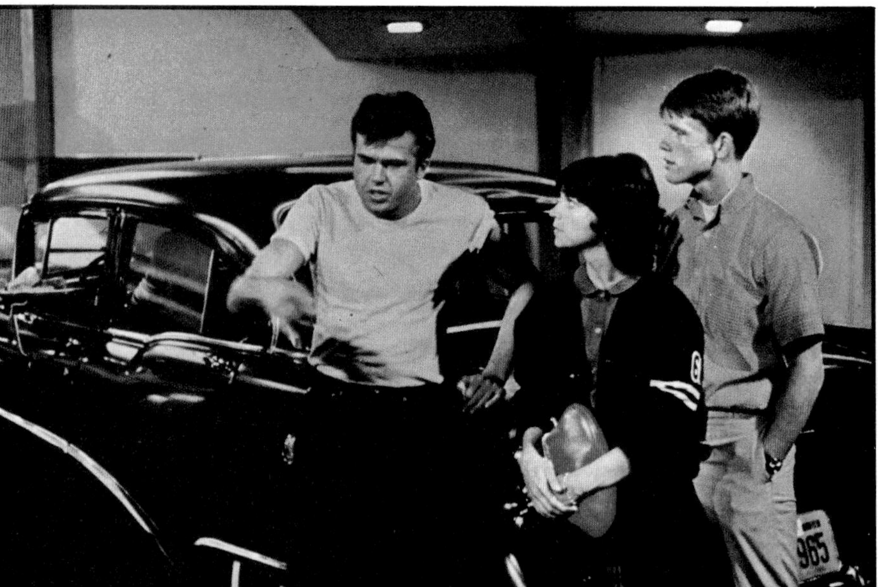

Celluloid Rock 1

(Specialist; worth 3 points each)

A) Name this movie.

B) Who are the actors pictured left to right ?

C) Which Rock 'n' Roll revival group appeared in the film ?

D) Who directed the movie ?

E) Which DJ featured in it ?

F) Under which label was the soundtrack released ?

9 Starfile/Buddy Holly

(Specialist; worth 3 points each)

A) Where and when was **Buddy Holly** born?
B) Who was his partner in a country music duo?
C) What was the name of his first record label?
D) Where did his first recording session take place?
E) Name the individual **Three Tunes.**
F) Who became **Buddy's** manager and producer in '57?
G) Under what name was *That'll Be The Day* released (on the **Coral** label)?
H) Who did he marry in '58?
I) Name his solo UK number one hit single.
J) What was his posthumous hit penned by **Chuck Berry**?

Below: Billy Fury (see 10. F)

10 They were really Rockin' in Bolton

(Specialist; worth 3 points each)

A) Born in Lucknow, India, he has become one of the music world's most enduring stars. Who is he ?

B) What were **The Shadows** originally called, and who was in their 1960 line-up ?

C) In '61 who took us *Halfway to Paradise* ?

D) Who penned *Shakin' All Over* ? What name did the composer sing under ?

E) Under what name is **Marty Wilde** known in the US ?

F) In what films did **Billy Fury** portray the rock stars **Stormy Tempest** and **Billy Universe** ?

G) By what name is **Tommy Hicks** better known ?

H) Under what title did **The Cougars** release an up-date of Tchaikovsky's *Swan Lake* ?

I) Who did **Shane Fenton** later become ?

J) In what TV series did **Jess Conrad** make his acting debut ?

K) Who in '62 had *A Picture of You* ?

L) Between leaving **The Shadows** and teaming up with **Tony Meeham, Jet Harris** scored with two hits. What were their titles ?

M) Where was writer/producer **Joe Meek's** hit-making studio ?

N) Name **The Tornados'** ex-bassist and the title of his hit tribute to **Eddie Cochran.**

O) Who penned **The Shadows'** *Apache* and *Wonderful Land*, and **Jet and Tony's** *Diamonds* and *Scarlett O'Hara* ?

P) In which film did **Adam Faith** co-star with **Shirley Ann Field** and **Oliver Reed** ?

Q) Where was the famous 2 I's coffee bar Rock 'n' Roll venue ?

R) Name **The Brook Brothers** and their biggest hit.

Left: The Tornados (*see* 10. N & V)

S) Who recorded the *Some People* movie soundtrack?
T) What was the cartoon character in TV's *Discs A-Go-Go*?
U) Who was the famous manager/impresario who handled such names as **Vince Eager, Dickie Pride, Johnny Gentle** and **Duffy Power**?
V) What was **The Tornados'** joint US and UK number one?
W) Who played the lead in the film *The Golden Disc*?
X) What was the title of TV's *Juke Box Jury* theme?
Y) Name the backing groups of:
1. **Marty Wilde**
2. **Tommy Bruce**
3. **Johnny Kidd**
4. **Mike Berry**
5. **Shane Fenton**

Z) Name the dynamic producer of such shows as *Oh Boy!* and *Boy Meets Girls.*

11 Who's Who in Rock Movies

(General; worth 2 points each)

From Presley to Travolta, rock movies have been a celluloid favourite for well over two decades. Name the main rock/pop stars of:

A) Remember Me This Way
B) April Love
C) Bird on a Wire
D) Harum Scarum
E) Play it Cool
F) O Lucky Man
G) Son of Dracula
H) Twist Around the Clock
I) Catch Us if You can (US title: Having a Wild Weekend)
J) Come September
K) Born to Boogie
L) Grease
M) Hound-Dog Man
N) Kona Coast
O) Mahogany
P) Imagine
Q) Follow the Boys
R) The Fastest Guitar Alive
S) Gidget
T) Ferry 'Cross the Mersey
U) I'd Rather be Rich
V) Serious Charge
W) Don't Look Back
X) Ballad in Blue
Y) Alice's Restaurant
Z) Bye Bye Birdie

12 Oscar Winning Hits

(Specialist; worth 3 points each)

These songs have all been nominated for an Oscar by the Academy of Motion Pictures.

Identify the winning entries and name their composers.

A) **1969**
Come Saturday Morning
(from *The Sterile Cuckoo*)
Raindrops Keep Falling On my Head
(from *Butch Cassidy and the Sundance Kid*)
True Grit
(from *True Grit*)
What Are You Doing the Rest of Your Life?
(from *The Happy Ending*)

B) **1971**
The Age of Not Believing
(from *Bedknobs and Broomsticks*)
All His Children
(from *Sometimes a Great Notion*)
Bless The Beasts & Children
(from *Bless the Beasts & Children*)
Life Is What You Make It
(from *Kotch*)
Theme from Shaft
(from *Shaft*)

20th CENTURY-FOX presents
BUTCH CASSIDY AND THE SUNDANCE KID

Right: Ritchie Valens (see 13. L)

13 Hail, Hail, Rock 'n' Roll
(Specialist; worth 3 points each)

A) Who wrote *The Book of Love*?
B) What instrument is **Sandy Nelson** famous for?
C) At the age of eighteen **Jack Scott** led which Detroit-based group?
D) Who was **The Dinning Sisters'** brother, and what was his biggest hit?
E) Where did **Norman Petty** set up his hit-making recording studio?
F) By what names are **Ray Hildebrand** and **Gill Jackson** better known?
G) Name the four movies in which **Eddie Cochran** appeared.
H) Who sang bass on **Johnny Cymbal's** *Hey Mr. Bassman*?
I) Which West Coast record label was formed by **Bob Keene**?
J) What disc is **Chan Romero** best remembered for?
K) Who in 1960 scored with *Poetry In Motion*?
L) How old was **Ritchie Valens** at the time of his death?
M) Where was **Gene Vincent** born?
N) Between June '57 and April '58 **Larry Williams** had four major US hits and three of them had girls' names in the titles. Name them.
O) When were **The Ventures** formed?
P) Where is **Link Wray's** legendary chicken coop recording studio?

Q) Name **Johnny and The Hurricanes'** first release.
R) Which **Doo-Wop** groups would you associate with the following hits?
1. *Sixteen Candles*
2. *Young Blood*
3. *Why Do Fools Fall In Love?*
4. *Blue Moon*
5. *Since I Don't Have You*
6. *Whispering Bells*
7. *Maybe*
8. *Angels in the Sky*
9. *Goodnight, Well It's time To Go*
10. *I'll Be Seeing You*

S) Who penned **The Fleetwood's** *The Great Imposter* hit?
T) What were **The Coasters** originally called?
U) Who is known as **Little Miss Dynamite**?
V) Name the record which launched **Roy Orbison's** career.
W) Individually, **Frankie Avalon** and **Fabian** have made movies with **John Wayne.** Name them.
X) Who played sax on **Buddy Holly's** *Early In the Morning*?
Y) What was on the B-side of **Bobby Darin's** *Dream Lover* hit?
Z) **Larry Williams** was once a member of which Rock 'n' Roller's backing group?

14 Starfile/Pat Boone

(Specialist; worth 3 points each)

A) Name the famous frontiersman from whom **Pat** is directly descended.

B) In which '54 talent competition did he win top honours?

C) Who signed **Pat** to the **Dot** record label?

D) What was the title of his '55 debut disc?

E) Who was his female co-star in *April Love*?

F) Name the four US number one hit singles he notched-up between '56 and '61.

G) In which movie based on a **Jules Verne** novel did he star in 1960?

H) What was the title of his joint US/UK '62 top ten single?

I) Who produced his '64 *Beach Girl* minor success?

J) Pat signed to the country music label **Melodyland** in Nashville. Name **Melodyland's** parent company.

Below: The Everly Brothers (*see* 15. J) Right: The Osmond brothers (*see* 16. E)

15 Hail, Hail, Rock 'n' Roll

(Specialist; worth 3 points each)

A) What was the title of **Ricky Nelson's** family TV show?

B) Who took **Charlie Gracie's** *Big Butterfly* hit even further up the charts?

C) The founders of **Cameo Records, Bernie Lowe** and **Kal Mann,** penned a big hit for **Presley**. What was its title?

D) Where was **Cameo Records** based?

E) What TV play helped launch **Tommy Sands'** singing career?

F) What was the title of **Ed (Kookie) Byrnes'** solo chart outing?

G) On what label was **The Ventures'** *Walk, Don't Run* originally released?

H) Who in '57 had a *Whole Lotta Shakin' Goin' On*?

I) In *Summertime Blues* where was **Eddie Cochran** going to take his problems?

J) Who penned a good majority of the **Everly Brothers'** hits, including *Bye Bye Love* and *Wake Up Little Susie*?

K) How many miles was it to the **Four Preps'** *Santa Catalina*?

L) Songwriter **Sharon Sheeley** was the fiancée of what late star?

M) Where was **Paul Anka** born?

N) As a D.J. **The Big Bopper** set a record for continuous broadcasting; how long did it last and what did he call his marathon?

O) What was **Frankie Avalon's** film debut?

P) Who scored in '58 with *When*?

Q) **Little Willie John** was famous for two big hits. What were they?

R) Who penned the instrumental hit, *Peter Gun*?

S) What was **Freddy Cannon's** nickname?

T) Who was **The Belmonts'** lead singer?

U) Name **Dickey Doo's** backing group.

V) How many *Little Girls* were "sitting in the back seat" with **Paul Evans** in '59?

W) What was the original title of *Kansas City*?

X) Who had a million-seller with *Here Comes Summer*?

Y) **Bobby Rydell** and **Frankie Avalon** both played in the same Philly group. What was it called?

Z) Who sang *Because They're Young*?

The Beatles

16 Rock All-Sorts

(General; worth 2 points each)

A) Name (full names) **The Walker Brothers**.

B) Who in '77 invited us to the *Hotel California*?

C) What dance craze is associated with the **Peppermint Lounge**?

D) Who formed **A & M Records**?

E) Name **Marie Osmond's** brothers.

F) **The Who** paid tribute to **The Rolling Stones** by recording two of their songs; what were they and when were they released?

G) What was **Ray Stevens'** debut single?

H) The following songs are about places. Where would you find them?
  1. **George Harrison's** *Blue Jay Way*
  2. **Gerry Rafferty's** *Baker Street*
  3. **Fred Neil's** *Bleeker and MacDougal*
  4. **Lennon/McCartney's** *Penny Lane*

I) The melody of **Mary Hopkins'** *Those were the Days* was based on what Russian folk song?

J) **Glen Campbell** was briefly a member of what major West Coast group?

K) Who produced **Nancy Sinatra's** *These Boots are Made for Walkin'* hit?

L) What was the name of **Deborah Harry's** first band?

M) Where was **Eddie and the Hotrods'** live EP recorded?

N) **Billy J. Kramer's** backing group scored with an instrumental. Name the group and the hit.

O) Who took *Wooden Heart* to the top of the US charts?

P) What have **Maurice Williams and The Zodiacs, The Hollies** and **Jackson Browne** in common?

Q) Who in '77 was *Foot Loose and Fancy Free*?

R) Where was the '78 **Front Row Festival** held?

S) Who were **Dirk, Nasty, Stig** and **Barry**?

T) What is **George Harrison's** record label called?

U) Where does **Dave Edmunds** hail from?

V) In what '71 major movie were **The Three Degrees** guest stars?

W) Who in '61 had *A Hundred Pounds of Clay*?

X) If you were going to San Francisco in '67 what would you be sure to wear?

Y) *City Riot, Al Capone* and *Burke's Law* were all Ska hits for what Jamaican group?

Z) What was the first song to be played on BBC's Radio One?

17 Superstars/The Beatles

(Specialist; worth 3 points each)

In the sixties, The Beatles were probably the most famous and popular men of the decade. Having carried all before them as a group, they then became four highly individual superstars of the seventies.

A) What year did **John** form **The Quarrymen** skiffle group?

B) Name the individual members of **The Silver Beatles.**

C) What instrument did one-time group member **Thomas Moore** play?

D) Who engaged the group as a supporting act on a Scottish tour headed by **Johnny Gentle**?

E) Who produced their early discs?

F) When did **Brian Epstein** sign **The Beatles**?

G) When did **Ringo** join the line-up, and of what Liverpool group had he been a member?

H) Who signed them to a recording contract, and to what company?

I) What was the title of their British debut disc?

J) Who topped the bill on their first national tour?

K) Their next single, *Please Please Me,* started a chain of **Beatles** UK number ones. What single split that chain?

L) What were the titles of **John's** two sixties books? Give their respective years of first publication.

M) Name the only two instrumentals **The Beatles** recorded throughout their career.

N) When did they appear in the

Royal Variety Show ?

O) Who was the first American to record a **Lennon/ McCartney** song, and what was its title ?

P) How many people applied for the 728 available seats at their debut US TV show, and who was their host ?

Q) Where did **George** meet **Pattie Boyd**?
R) Who directed their two movies, *A Hard Day's Night* and *Help*?
S) Which three members of **The Rolling Stones** gatecrashed their *Hard Day's Night* premiere party?
T) What were they awarded in '65 that brought a storm of protest from existing award holders?
U) Name the title of their first US number one hit and its B-side.
V) At what New York sports arena did they play to capacity audiences in '65 and '66?
W) Name the track and the UK album on which **Ringo** made his vocal debut.
X) Where was their last live UK performance?
Y) On what '64 **Alma Cogan** disc is **Paul** credited as playing tambourine?
Z) Who was quoted as saying "**The Beatles** are now more popular than Christ"?

18 Encore Quiz/The Beatles

(Specialist; worth 3 points each)

A) What did the New York disc jockey **Murray the K** claim to be in February '64?
B) Under what pseudonyms was **Paul** credited as composer of **Peter and Gordon's** *Woman* hit?
C) Who taught **George** to play the sitar?
D) Why was *A Day In the Life* banned by the BBC and some US stations?
E) When did they appear on the live world-wide satellite TV show *Our World*, and what did they perform?
F) Where were **The Beatles** when **Brian Epstein** died from an overdose of drugs?
G) Name the Guru they became associated with.
H) What was the title of the

movie in which **John** made his solo acting debut ?

I) Where was their clothing store ?

J) Who in '68 became their press officer for the second time ?

K) When did **Paul** marry **Linda** and **John** marry **Yoko** ?

L) Which two **Beatles** failed to appear on *The Ballad of John and Yoko* single ?

M) Who played key-boards on their *Get Back* hit ?

N) What was the title of the movie in which **Ringo** portrayed a gardener ?

O) When was their *Magical Mystery Tour* TV film premièred ?

P) Who directed the animated cartoon feature *Yellow Submarine* ?

Q) What were the titles of the previously unreleased songs on the *Yellow Submarine* soundtrack ?

R) Name the song titles of the first release on **The Beatles' Apple** label.

S) What was the title of the B-side of *Ticket To Ride* ?

T) Who released a single under the name **Muskateer Gripweed** ?

U) Where was their final US live performance ?

V) Apart from the title track, what songs appeared on the UK *Long Tall Sally* extended play ?

W) Who directed the *Let It Be* movie ?

X) On what album did *Across The Universe* first appear ?

Y) Who was appointed their adviser in February '69 ?

Z) What was the title of the last album they recorded together ?

19 Mystery Openers

(General; worth 2 points each)

Name the titles of the opening tracks on the following albums:

A) **Aretha Franklin's** *Now* ('68)

B) **Randy Newman's** *Little Criminals* ('77)

C) **Barbara Streisand's** *Songbird* ('78)

D) **Area Code 615's** *Trip In The Country* ('70)

E) **The Beatles'** *At the Hollywood Bowl* ('77)

F) **The Doors'** *Waiting For the Sun* ('68)

G) **Ry Cooder's** *Chicken Skin Music* ('76)

H) **Santana's** *Abraxas* ('70)

I) **Nick Lowe's** *Jesus of Cool* ('78)

J) **Bob Dylan's** *Highway 61 Revisited* ('65)

K) **The Rolling Stones'** *Some Girls* ('78)

L) **Neil Young's** *Comes A Time* ('78)

M) **Sylvester's** *Step II* ('78)

N) **Isaac Hayes'** *Chocolate Chip* ('75)

O) **10 cc's** *The Original Soundtrack* ('75)

P) **Delaney and Bonnie's** *Accept No Substitute* ('69)

Q) **The Shadows'** *The Shadows* ('61)

R) **Otis Redding's** *Otis Blue* ('66)

S) **The Beach Boys'** *Sunflower* ('70)

T) **Jackson Browne's** *The Pretender* ('76)

U) **The Everly Brothers'** *The New Album* ('77)

V) **Fleetwood Mac's** *Rumours* ('77)

W) **The Ramones'** *Road to Ruin* ('78)

X) **John Lennon's** *Walls and Bridges* ('74)

Y) **Elvis Costello's** *This Year's Model* ('78)

Z) **Bob Seeger and The Silver Bullet Band's** *Night Moves* ('76)

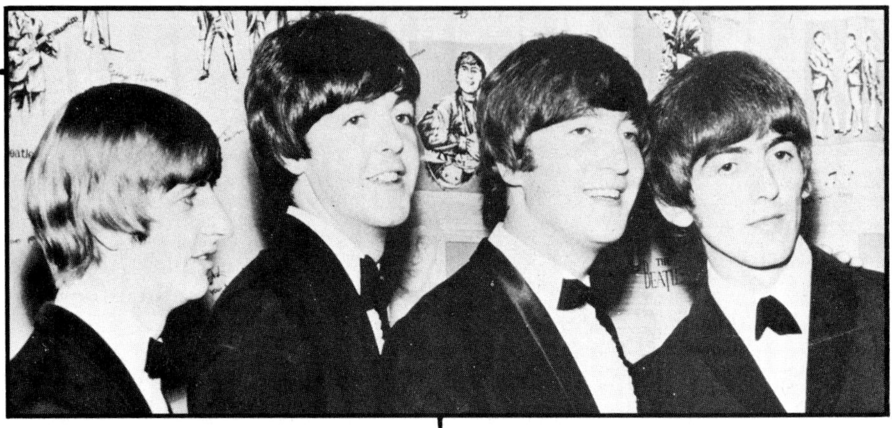

20 Beatle Music Puzzle

(Specialist; worth 3 points each)

A) **During their prolific songwriting partnership, John Lennon and Paul McCartney composed the majority of The Beatles' recorded work. Can you identify the non-Lennon/McCartney songs from this list of Beatles' records ?**

1. *Please Please Me*
2. *Twist and Shout*
3. *Little Child*
4. *Devil In Her Heart*
5. *Eight Days A Week*
6. *Ticket To Ride*
7. *Drive My Car*
8. *Good Day Sunshine*
9. *Something*
10. *One After 909*

B) Which song did **Ringo** contribute to the *Abbey Road* album ?

C) What did **Bungalow Bill** go out tiger hunting with ?

D) In *Cry, Baby, Cry* where did the duchess who was always smiling come from ?

E) What three songs on the UK *Revolver* album did **George Harrison** contribute ?

F) Where did the dirty man's son work in *Paperback Writer* ?

G) In *A Day In The Life* how many holes were there in Blackburn, Lancashire ?

H) Who penned *Act Naturally*, included on the UK *Help* album and on the US *Yesterday and Today* album ?

I) What's on the corner of *Penny Lane* ?

J) In *Hey Bulldog* what is frightened of the dark ?

K) What song from what album is credited to **Lennon/McCartney/Starkey** ?

L) In *She's Leaving Home*, where is she on Friday morning at nine o'clock ?

M) What is the title of the **George Harrison** song included in the movie *Sergeant Pepper's Lonely Hearts Club Band* ?

N) Who were kicking **Edgar Allen Poe** in *I Am The Walrus* ?

O) Name the titles of the songs **John, Paul** and **George** provided individually for **Ringo's** '73 *Ringo* album ?

P) Who was jointly credited as producing the *Let It Be* album ?

Q) What is the full title of **Lennon/McCartney's** *I Want You* ?

R) Name **The Beatles'** album tracks the following acts covered as hit singles :

1. **The Overlanders**
2. **St. Louis Union**
3. **Silkie**
4. **The Hollies**
5. **Young Idea**
6. **Cliff Bennett and The Rebel Rousers**
7. **Jan and Dean**
8. **Kenny Ball and his Jazzmen**
9. **Billy J. Kramer and The Dakotas**
10. **Marmalade**

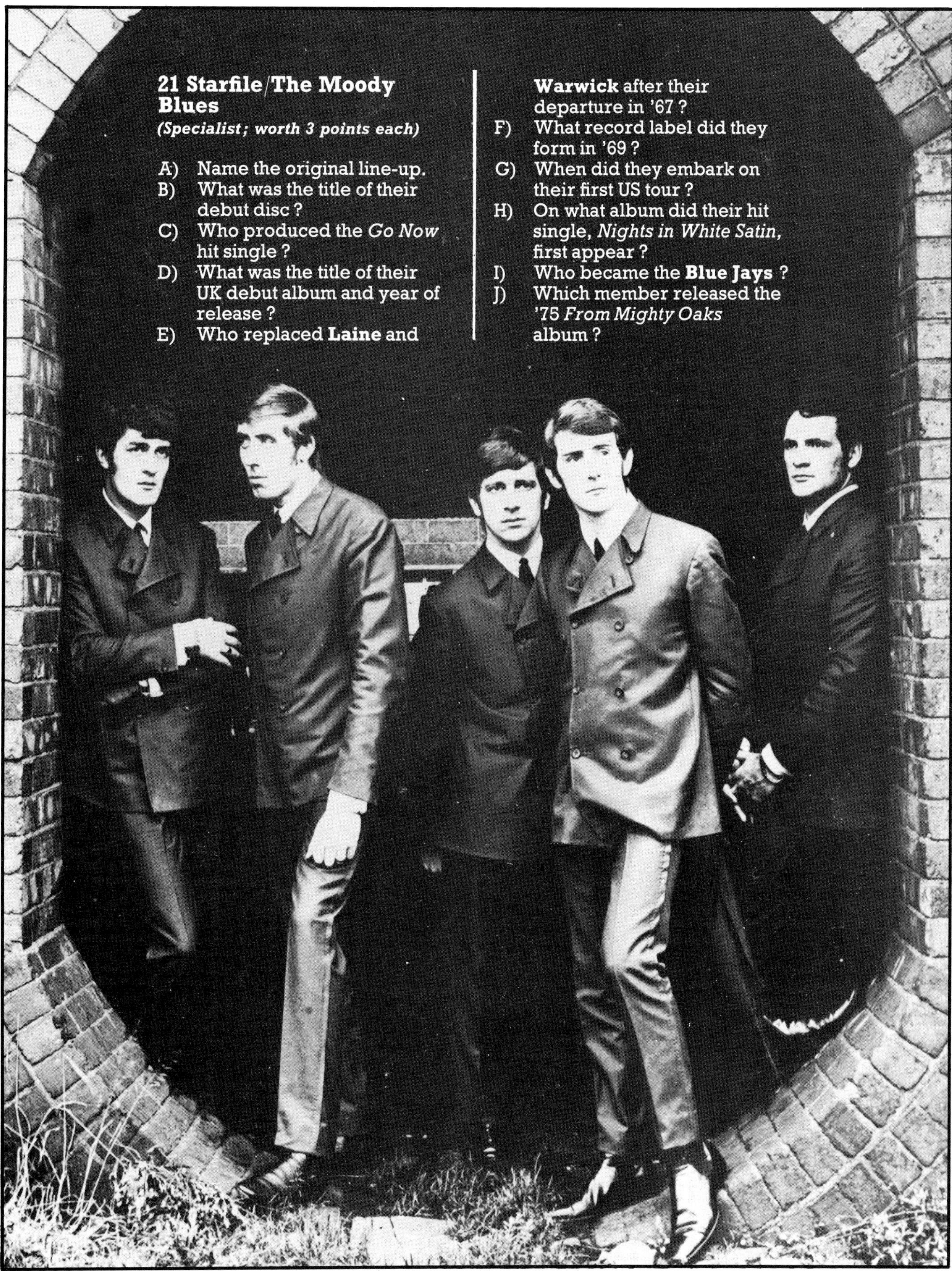

21 Starfile/The Moody Blues

(Specialist; worth 3 points each)

A) Name the original line-up.
B) What was the title of their debut disc?
C) Who produced the *Go Now* hit single?
D) What was the title of their UK debut album and year of release?
E) Who replaced **Laine** and **Warwick** after their departure in '67?
F) What record label did they form in '69?
G) When did they embark on their first US tour?
H) On what album did their hit single, *Nights in White Satin*, first appear?
I) Who became the **Blue Jays**?
J) Which member released the '75 *From Mighty Oaks* album?

Right: Richard Chamberlain (see 22. T)

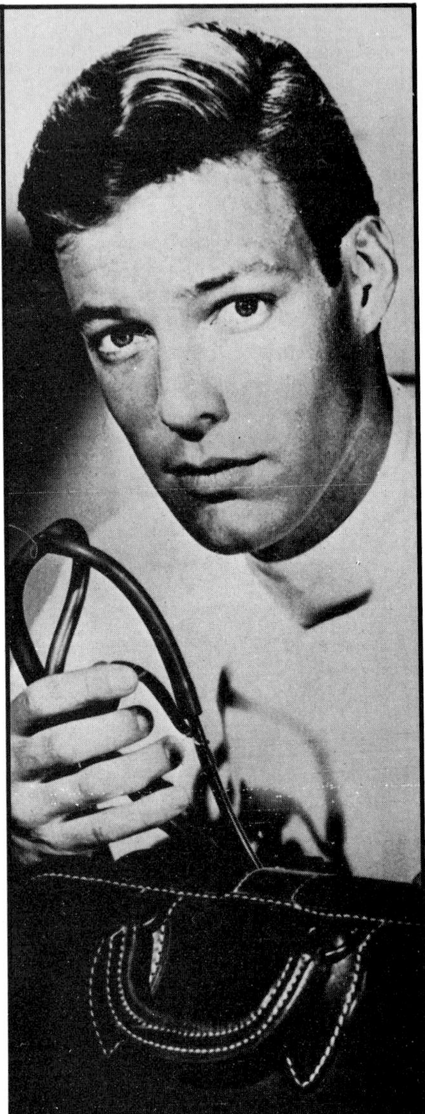

Picture Quiz 2
(Specialist; worth 3 points each)

From 1941 to the early seventies the Ryman Auditorium (above) **played host to a famous show of a certain musical style.**

A) What was the name of the show ?
B) What was the musical style ?
C) In what city was it situated ?

22 Rock All-Sorts
(General; worth 2 points each)

A) Who sang *Nilsson sings Newman* ?
B) What was **Unit Four Plus Two's** big '65 hit ?
C) Who in '75 was *Wide Eyed and Legless* ?
D) What nationality were **The Spotnicks** ?
E) How old was **Paul Anka** at the time of his *Diana* hit ?
F) A Chicago banker, Gen. Charles Gates Dawes, composed a simple melody he entitled *Melody In A Major*. It has since been a hit for a host of stars including **Cliff Richard, Tommy Edwards** and **The Four Tops.** Under what title is the song better known ?
G) Who cut the original version of *Lucky Lips* (made popular by **Cliff Richard**) ?
H) His vocal style (spanning some twenty years) has been tagged 'Makeout Music'. Who is he ?
I) What question did **Lonnie Donegan** ask in '59 ?
J) Where was *The Beach Boys Live in London* recorded ?
K) When was *Oh Pretty Woman* a big hit for **Roy Orbison** ?
L) A former Australian child actor was once a member of **The Bee Gees.** What is his name ?
M) **Tab Hunter** in '57 and **Donny Osmond** in '73 both made the number one spot with the same song. What is its title ?
N) Who sang with **The Union Gap** ?
O) What hit-making Irish group was fronted by **Van Morrison** ?
P) Which songwriting team penned **Sweet's** first dozen hits ?
Q) **Eric Stewart** of **10cc** fame was once the lead guitarist/vocalist of what hit sixties Manchester group ?
R) Who was **The Tremeloes'** original lead singer ?
S) Where did **The Dave Clark**

Five hail from ?

T) What was actor **Richard Chamberlain's** biggest hit ?

U) The group **Man** were originally known as **The Bystanders.** Where were they formed and what was their sole hit single ?

V) Who scored in '79 with *I Was Made For Dancing* ?

W) What was the title of **The Walker Brothers'** '76 comeback hit ?

X) Which group made a guest appearance in **Michelangelo Antonioni's** movie *Blow Up* ?

Y) Who in '79 revived **Reparata and The Delrons'** *Captain of Your Ship* ?

Z) What is **Donovan's** surname ?

23 Starfile/The Who

(Specialist; worth 3 points each)

A) Name the original line-up.

B) Where did **Keith Moon** meet the group ?

C) What UK youth cult were they closely identified with ?

D) Who produced their early discs ?

E) What was the title of their debut single ?

F) Name the instrumental track included on the *My Generation* album .

G) Who penned *Boris The Spider* ?

H) What famous film maker directed the movie version of **Pete Townshend's** rock opera *Tommy* ?

I) Where was their live album recorded ?

J) Who replaced **Keith Moon** after his tragic death in '78 ?

Right: The Small Faces (*see* 24. F)

24 The Beat Scene: UK Rock in the Sixties

(Specialist; worth 3 points each)

A) Name the trio of '63 singles **Gerry and The Pacemakers** took to the UK number one spot in quick succession.

B) What group did **Peter Noone** front?

C) Where did **The Animals** hail from?

D) By what name did **Tommy Scott** of **The Senators** become better known?

E) What famous detective theme did **Freddie Starr** turn into a *Loco-Motion*?

F) Name the individual members of **The Small Faces.**

Celluloid Rock 2

(Specialist; worth 3 points each)

A) Name this **Beatles** movie.

B) Who directed the film?

C) Who portrayed the High Priest Clang?

D) When (full date) was the movie premiered?

E) Who portrayed the lost swimmer in the foreground of this still?

F) Which US label issued the soundtrack?

G) Who replaced **Paul Jones** after his departure from the **Manfred Mann** group ?

H) When was *Little Children* a top ten hit in both the US and the UK for **Billy J. Kramer** ?

I) What group scored in '65 with *It's Good News Week* ?

J) **Jefferson** (once the lead singer of **The Rockin' Berries**) made the charts with what '69 hit ?

K) Which group did **Dave Berry** sing with ?

L) In what Hammer horror movie were **Amen Corner** guest stars ?

M) What was the title of **The Dave Clark Five's** '65 US number one hit single ?

N) Who produced **Cilla Black's** big hits ?

O) What was the title of **Alan Price's** first solo single ?

P) Name the individual members of the original **Kinks.**

Q) From where did **The Searchers** get their name ?

R) What was **The Hollies'** debut single ?

S) Who introduced **The Freddie** dance craze in '65 ?

T) Where did **Bern Elliot and The Fenmen** hail from ?

U) In what Liverpool club did **Cilla Black** work as a hatcheck girl ?

V) Who penned **The Fourmost's** *Hello, Little Girl* and *I'm In Love* ?

W) When was *Tobacco Road* a US/UK hit for **The Nashville Teens** ?

X) **The Sorrows** scored in the UK with *Take a Heart* in '65, but where were they even more successful ?

Y) What big line-up instrumental group backed most visiting US rock stars in the mid-sixties while also scoring with *The Spartans* single ?

Z) By what name did **Cass and the Casanovas** become better known ?

25 Who are they ?

(General; worth 2 points each)

Those listed below achieved fame under new names. What are their star names ?

A) Al Cernik
B) Eric Hilliard Nelson
C) Terence Harris
D) Bobby Velline
E) Ruth Jones
F) Brian Alford and Colin Day
G) Richard Starkey
H) Jean Phillippe Smet
I) James Ercolaui
J) Eva Narcissus Boyd
K) Gary Anderson
L) William Ashton
M) Steven Judkins
N) Eugene Dixon
O) Priscilla Maria Veronica White
P) Clive Powell
Q) Christopher Montanez
R) Brian Hines
S) Leonard Borisoff
T) Glyn Geoffrey Ellis
U) Domingo Sumudio
V) Sharon Myers
W) Thomas Jones Woodward
X) Florence Bisenta de Casilles Martinez Cardona
Y) Terence Nelhams
Z) Ronald Wycherley

26 Superstars/The Rolling Stones

(Specialist; worth 3 points each)

For almost two decades The Rolling Stones have been reelin' and a rockin' between triumphs, tragedies and tuning-up. They are surely the best Rock 'n' Roll band in the world.

A) When were **The Rolling Stones** formed ?
B) Who became their manager on April 29, 1963 ?
C) Name the original line-up.
D) Give the title of their first single release.
E) When, and on what show, did they make their UK TV debut ?
F) Who did they support on their first UK tour ?
G) What **Beatle** song did they cover ?

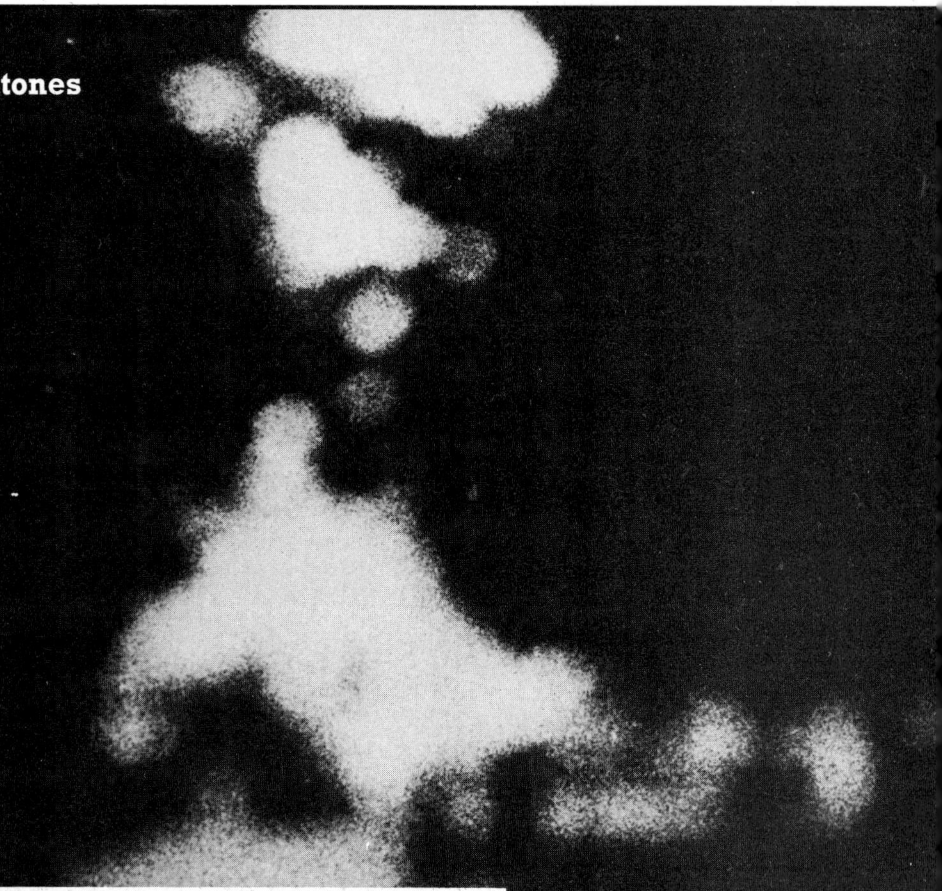

Picture Quiz 3

(Specialist; worth 3 points each)

A) Identify **The Rolling Stones'** two friends pictured here.

B) Which track on which **Rolling Stones'** album was dedicated to them?

C) The celebrity seated played piano on a track recorded by **The Stones.** What was its title and who were credited as composers?

D) Which member of **The Ronettes** married the friend pictured far left?

H) Who recorded **Jagger** and **Richard's** *That Girl Belongs To Yesterday*?

I) What was the title of their first US single release and who had originally recorded it?

J) **Charlie Watts** wrote and illustrated a book entitled *Ode To A High Flying Bird.* Who was it about?

K) Give the title of their first joint US/UK number one hit single.

L) In which '64 US rock concert movie did they appear?

M) Who became their co-manager in August '65?

N) With what **Jagger/Richard** composition did **Marianne Faithful** score in both the UK and US Charts?

O) Where was the **Stones'** first concert behind the Iron Curtain?

P) Name the single on which **John Lennon** and **Paul McCartney** supplied background vocals.

Q) What was the title of their (never shown) TV film, directed by **Michael Lindsay-Hogg**?

R) When did **Brian Jones** quit **The Stones**?

S) Name the single on which **Mick Taylor** made his debut.

T) When (full date) was **Brian** found dead at his home?

U) In what movie did **Mick Jagger** make his acting debut?

V) Where was **Mick's** *Ned Kelly* film premiered?

W) Who (full name) did **Mick Jagger** marry on May 12, 1971?

X) What was the first single on **The Rolling Stones Records** label?

Y) Who designed the sleeve of the first album on **The Rolling Stones Records** label and what was its title?

Z) Who replaced **Mick Taylor** after he departed in '74?

27 Rock All-Sorts

(General; worth 2 points each)

A) Give the title of **Simon and Garfunkel's** '75 reunion single.
B) Where was **The Plastic Ono Band's** *Give Peace A Chance* recorded?
C) Name the individual members of the original **Lovin' Spoonful.**
D) Which ex-member of **The McCoys** released a solo version of their *Hang On Sloopy* in '75?
E) **Dorothy Provine** scored a big hit in '61 partly helped by the popularity of her TV series. Name the hit and the show.
F) Who formed the **Red Bird** label?
G) What was the title of **The Ramrods'** sole hit?

H) Who partnered **Mike Sarne** on 1. *Come Outside* and 2. *Will I What?*
I) Name **Tommy Roe's** two US number one hit singles.
J) What is the title of **Rolling Stone Bill Wyman's** '76 solo album?
K) Brooklyn's *Odyssey 2001 Club* was the background in which big disco movie?
L) Who were *Up Town Top Ranking*?
M) Name the movie in which **Leif Garrett** made his acting debut.
N) **Frank Farian** is the creator, writer and producer behind what seventies disco supergroup?
O) Who are **The Glimmer Twins**?
P) What was the title of **Cat Stevens'** debut disc?
Q) On **The Who's** *Who Are You* album cover, what does the notice say on **Keith Moon's** chair?
R) Who scored in '67 with *Gimme Little Sign*?
S) Which UK girl singer has achieved a record of three number one hit singles?
T) Name the singer of *Itsy Bitsy Teeny Weeny Yellow Polkadot Bikini* and *Lop-Sided, Over-Loaded And It Wiggled When We Rode It.*
U) In what movie did **Tab Hunter** and **Fabian** co-star?
V) Who scored in '58 with *Born Too Late*?
W) Name the group **Emitt Rhodes** fronted in '67.
X) Give the title of **Zager and Evans'** one-off hit.
Y) How many UK number one hits has **Frank Ifield** to his credit?
Z) Which TV detective scored with *Don't Give Up On Us* in '76?

28 Starfile/Jimi Hendrix

(Specialist; worth 3 points each)

A) Which famous singing brothers employed **Jimi** in '64?
B) Where, and in what year, was the **Hendrix/Curtis Knight** album recorded?
C) When were **The Experience** formed and who were brought in on bass and drums?
D) Give the title of **Jimi's** first UK top ten hit single.
E) Where was he jailed in '68 for wrecking his hotel room?
F) When did **The Experience** officially disband?
G) What mammoth festival did **Jimi** play at in June '69?
H) Where was the *Band of Gypsies* album recorded?
I) Why was his 1970 European tour cancelled?
J) What was the date of **Jimi Hendrix's** tragic death?

29 Black Music

(Specialist; worth 3 points each)

For decades, black rhythms and styles have been a most influential contribution to the world of popular music and have formed the basis of rock itself.

A) Who called **Otis** a *Tramp*?
B) Where is the *Apollo Theatre* located?
C) Who was **R.B.** (*Take a letter, Maria*) **Greaves'** famous uncle?
D) What do the initials **M.G.** of **Booker T and the M.G.s** fame stand for?
E) Who was **Fontella Bass's** partner on *Don't Mess up a Good Thing*?
F) He has been described as America's greatest living poet. Who is he?
G) What was the title of **The Toys'** big '67 hit and what melody was it based on?
H) By what name is **Robert Higgenbotham** better known, and what is the title of his much covered '64 hit?
I) Where were the famous **Stax** studios located?
J) Who is known as **Mr. TNT**?
K) What is **Ray Charles'** full name?
L) Who was the brain behind the rise of the **Tamla Motown Organization**?
M) Name **Tamla Motown's** first gold disc.
N) Name those who partnered **Marvin Gaye** on:
1. *Once Upon a Time*
2. *It Takes Two*
3. *Onion Song*
4. *You Are Everything*
O) **Aretha's** sister scored a hit in '67. Name her and the hit.
P) What big 70's writer/singer/producer co-produced **Bob and Earl's** *Harlem Shuffle*, and what are the duo's surnames?
Q) Name **The Jackson Brothers.**
R) Where was **Wilson Pickett** born, and who co-wrote his massive *Midnight Hour* hit?
S) What was **Tina Turner's** maiden name?
T) Who first recorded *The Twist*?
U) In what film did **Billy Preston** play the part of **W.C. Handy**?
V) Under what name did **Otis Redding** release his first single, what was its title and year of release?
W) What are **Sam and Dave's** full names?
X) **Stax** is a combination of whose names?
Y) He has produced **Al Green and Ann Peebles** and made records as **The Bill Black Combo.** Who is he?
Z) Name the individual members of **Boney M.**

30 Starfile/Otis Redding

(Specialist; worth 3 points each)

A) Where was **Otis** born?
B) With what group did he work as a roadie?
C) Who at **Stax Records** signed him to a recording deal in '62?
D) On what label did his *These Arms of Mine* first appear?
E) Name the UK group who helped spread his name by recording his '63 hit *Pain In My Heart.*
F) Who co-wrote his *I've Been Loving You Too Long (To Stop Now)*?
G) Which movie captured a special '67 live performance?
H) Name the **Beatle** song which **Otis** included on his *Dictionary of Soul* album.
I) How old was **Otis** at the time of his tragic death?
J) **Otis's** son released a single in '73 on the **Capricorn** label. What is his name and the title of the disc?

Right: The Tavares (see 31. D)

31 Black Music

(Specialist; worth 3 points each)

A) Who scored in '78 with *Love Don't Live Here Anymore*?

B) **Natalie Cole** is the daughter of which late great crooner?

C) What two **Lennon and McCartney** songs did **Ray Charles** take into the charts?

D) Name the individual **Tavares** brothers.

E) What was the title of **Otis Redding's** big posthumous hit?

F) Under what title was **Stevie Wonder** known at the start of his recording career?

G) Name the original lead singer with **The Detroit Spinners.**

H) What do the initials MFSB stand for?

I) On what album did *I Heard It Through the Grapevine* appear, performed by **Smokey Robinson and The Miracles**?

J) Which **Jackson** brother stayed at **Motown** after the group signed to **Epic** in '76?

K) Where was **Stevie Wonder's** *Fingertips* recorded?

L) Who led **The Impressions** after **Jerry Butler's** departure from the group?

M) What was **The Marvelettes'** follow-up to their hugely successful *Please Mr. Postman*?

N) By what name is **Desmond Dacres** better known?

O) Under what title did **Eddie Holman's** *Hey There Lonely Girl* first appear and who were the vocalists?

P) What group joined **Ramsey Lewis** and his '75 *Hot Dawgit* and *Sun Goddess* hits?

Q) Name the **Tamla Motown** acts you associate with these hits:
1. *Dancing In the Street*
2. *This Old Heart of Mine*
3. *I Was Made to Love Her*
4. *Ain't That Peculiar*
5. *Papa Was A Rollin' Stone*
6. *Shotgun*
7. *My Guy*
8. *You Keep Me Hangin' On*
9. *Reach Out, I'll Be There*
10. *Tears of a Clown*

R) What was **Max Romeo's** big '69 hit?

S) Who scored with *Dat* in '76?

T) The '71 *Soul to Soul* movie celebrated a national event. What was it?

U) With which New Orleans producers do you associate **The Meters, Lee Dorsey, Irma Thomas** and **Betty Harris**?

V) Who appeared in and wrote the soundtrack for the film *Sounder*?

W) What was **George McCrae's** big '74 disco hit?

X) Which group scored with the big double-sided *Rivers of Babylon/Brown Girl In The Ring* '78 hit?

Y) What was the title of **Chic's** debut single?

Z) Who produced **Candi Staton's** *Young Hearts Run Free* album?

32 Starfile/The Supremes

(Specialist; worth 3 points each)

A) What was the title of their first US pop chart entry ?

B) Name their joint US/UK number one hit single.

C) In which '64 rock concert movie did they appear ?

D) Who replaced the late **Florence Ballard** when she quit the original line-up ?

E) What was the title of the album which featured such songs as *How Do You Do It, Hard Day's Night, Bits and Pieces,* etc ?

F) Who did they remember with a '65 tribute album ?

G) **The Supremes** scored a hit with the title song from a movie starring **Anthony Quinn** and **Faye Dunaway.** Name the movie.

H) What was the title of the first single credited to **Diana Ross and The Supremes** ?

I) Who became the accepted leader after the departure of **Diana Ross,** and what was the new group's first single ?

J) In what movie did **Diana Ross** co-star with **Michael Jackson** and **Lena Horne** ?

Right: James Brown (*see* 33. G)

33 Black Music

(Specialist; worth 3 points each)

A) With what group did **Dionne Warwick** duet on the *Then Came You* hit?

B) **Sam Cooke's** brother penned his first million-seller. Name him and the hit.
C) By what name was **Curtis Ousley** better known?
D) In what TV private eye series did **Dionne Warwick** and **Isaac Hayes** guest star together?
E) Who died tragically as the result of playing Russian roulette?
F) Name the individual **Four Tops.**
G) Give the title of the record which launched **James Brown's** incredible career.
H) Who originally recorded *Night Train*?
I) What is the full title of **Sly and The Family Stone's** double-sided '69 hit?
J) Who discovered **The Jackson Five**?
K) In which film did **The Supremes** sing *Surfer Boy*?

L) What was **Johnny Taylor's** first single on the **Galaxy** label?
M) Who was the sole survivor of the **Otis Redding/Bar-Keys** air disaster?
N) *Cowboys to Girls* was a big hit for which Philly group?
O) What duo penned many of **The Stylistics'** hits, including *You Make Me Feel Brand New* and *You are Everything*?
P) Name **The Isley Brothers.**
Q) Who was the man from Trenchtown hailed as **The Black Bob Dylan**?
R) Before embarking on a solo career, **Ben E. King** sang lead with which durable group?

S) Name **Aretha Franklin's** first recording company.
T) Who scored in '67 with *Sweet Soul Music*?
U) What is **Vincent Montana's** *Dance Fantasy* based on?
V) In what '59 movie did **Johnny Nash** play the leading role?
W) Who has been labelled **'The Genius'**?
X) **Solomon Burke's** younger brothers, **Alex** and **Laddie,** were members of a one-hit group. Name the group and the hit.
Y) Name **Rufus Thomas's** big '63 hits and the dance craze they started.
Z) Who fronted the group **Rufus**?

34 Starfile/Booker T and The M.G.s

(Specialist; worth 3 points each)

A) When were **The M.G.s** formed?
B) Name the original bass player.
C) Which members had originally been with the **Mar-Keys** (of *Last Night* fame)?
D) What was the title of their first big hit?
E) Name the track and the album on which **Booker T** was first recorded playing piano.
F) What were the titles of their two Christmas singles, culled from the album *In The Xmas Spirit*?
G) On what movie soundtrack did their joint US/UK top ten single, *Time Is Tight*, feature?
H) Who replaced **Booker T** and **Steve Cropper** (for one album only) after their departure from the group?
I) What was the title of their '77 reunion album, and who was sadly missing from the original line-up?
J) Who is **Booker T's** rock singer wife?

Below: TV's Happy Days (*see* 35. V)

35 Rock All-Sorts

(General; worth 2 points each)

A) How does the *Easy Rider* soundtrack album differ from the film score?

B) What **Eddie Cochran** hit did **The Sex Pistols** revive in '79?

C) Who recorded *Sittin' on the Balcony* under the name **Johnny Dee**?

D) Name **Rod Stewart's** joint US and UK number one hit.

E) Where was **Jimi Hendrix** born, and what was his full name?

F) Which member of **The String-A-Longs** co-wrote

Sugar Shack, and what was the group's big '61 instrumental hit?

G) Who replaced **Eric Clapton** after he left **The Yardbirds**?

H) Where did **America** form?

I) **Ry Cooder** and **Queen** have both released albums under the same title. What is the title?

J) **Neil Diamond** penned two of **The Monkees'** biggest hits. Name them.

K) In what film did **Hayley Mills** sing her *Let's Get Together* hit?

L) Where is **The Kinks'** *Sunset*?

M) Under what name were **Creedance Clearwater Revival** originally known?

N) What group did **Norman** (*Spirit In the Sky*) **Greenbaum** front, and what was the title of their '66 hit?

O) Who scored with *Big Six, Big Seven* and *Big Eight*?

P) Name the groups of which **Crosby, Stills and Nash** were members before joining together in '68.

Q) In the early 60's **Johnny Crawford** scored with a string of hits, including *Cindy's Birthday* and

Rumors, and was also the star of a TV Western series. Name the series.

R) By what name is **Kent Lavoie** better known ?

S) Which three hit singles were culled from **The Four Seasons'** *Who Loves You* album ?

T) Name the title and act of **Elektra's** first single picture disc.

U) What were **Amen Corner** called after they dropped their brass section ?

V) Who made the charts with the title song from TV's *Happy Days* ?

W) Give the original title of **David Bowie's** *Space Oddity* album.

X) When (full date) was the TAMI show filmed ?

Y) Who in '77 recorded a double-sided single of some thirty **Beatle** songs ?

Z) In what '62 film did **Del**

Shannon perform *You Never Talked About Me* ?

Celluloid Rock 3

(Specialist; worth 3 points each)

A) Name this movie.

B) What stars are pictured in this still ?

C) Who directed the film ?

D) What year was the movie released ?

36 Rock Movie Stars

(General; worth 2 points each)

Name the following rock/pop stars of these movies:

A) Sergeant Pepper's Lonely Hearts Club Band
B) Carry It On
C) Babes in Toyland
D) Expresso Bongo
E) Girls Town
F) I'll Take Sweden
G) The Duke Wore Jeans
H) Head
I) Gimme Shelter
J) Lady Sings the Blues
K) High School Confidential
L) Adventures of the Son of Exploding Sausage
M) Hold On
N) Nashville Rebel
O) Mix Me a Person
P) That'll be the Day
Q) Privilege
R) Untamed Youth
S) I've Gotta Horse
T) Rainbow Bridge
U) Mad Dogs & Englishmen
V) Love & Kisses
W) Superfly
X) Pat Garrett and Billy the Kid
Y) Fun in Acapulco
Z) The Harder They Come

Picture Quiz 4

(Specialist; worth 3 points each)

A) Name the individuals pictured here.
B) Under what pseudonym were they credited for the '65 *I Want Candy* hit single?
C) Name their mid-sixties production company.
D) Which (later chart-topping) Indiana group did they discover in Dayton, Ohio?
E) What was the title of their hit song recorded by **The Merseys, David Bowie** and others?
F) Which member of the team later produced **Blondie's** debut album?

37 Oscar Winners

(Specialist; worth 3 points each)

Identify the winning entries and their composers.

A) 1966
Alfie
(from *Alfie*)
Born Free
(from *Born Free*)
Georgy Girl
(from *Georgy Girl*)
My Wishing Doll
(from *Hawaii*)
A Time for Love
(from *An American Dream*)

B) 1973
All That Love Went to Waste
(from *A Touch of Class*)
Live and Let Die
(from *Live and Let Die*)
Love
(from *Robin Hood*)

The Way We Were
(from *The Way We Were*)
Nice To Be Around
(from *Cinderella Liberty*)

38 Superstars/The Beach Boys

(Specialist; worth 3 points each)

The Beach Boys created their own highly distinctive West Coast sound, incorporating close harmonies, rolling melodies and brilliantly evocative songs, and earned themselves superstar status in the world of rock.

A) Name the original line-up.

B) Who did **David Marks** replace for a year?

C) What relation is **Mike Love** to the **Wilson Brothers**?

D) **Brian Wilson** wrote title songs for three **Beach** movies. What were they?

E) In what film did **The Beach Boys** co-star with **Lana Wood** and **Noreen Corcoran,** and who directed it?

F) Name the first album completely produced by **Brian Wilson.**

G) Before joining the group in '65 **Bruce Johnston** had been half of a surf music duo. Name the duo and give his partner's full name.

H) Under two group names **Brian Wilson** produced records by his wife and sister-in-law. What were the groups called and what are the ladies' names?

I) What is the title of the group's only joint US and UK number one hit single?

J) Name the group's ill-fated mid-sixties album that was never released.

K) Who was missing from the front cover pic on the *Summer Days Summer Nights* album sleeve?

L) What religious cult has been associated with the group?

M) Name **Brian Wilson's** LA health-food store.

N) What is the title of **The Beach Boys'** album of backing tracks?

O) Which member of the group co-starred with **James Taylor** in an auto movie, and what was the film's title?

P) Name the group's three Christmas singles.

Q) **Mike Love** has two brothers connected with the group in a behind-the-scenes role. Who are they?

R) What is the title of **Brian Wilson's** *Holland* fairytale?

S) Name the '76 **15 Big Ones** line-up and give their dates of birth.

Right: Carole King (see 40. U)

39 Who are they ?

(Specialist; worth 3 points each)

The following found fame under other names. By what names are they now known ?

A) Autney De Walt
B) James Marcus Smith
C) William Robinson
D) Peter Smith
E) Eunice Wayman
F) Cherilyn Sarkasian Lapier
G) Charles Hatcher
H) Tommy Montgomery
I) Herbert Khaury
J) Doris Payne
K) Riley King
L) Roy Charles Hammond
M) Don Van Vliet
N) Carol Hedges
O) David Harman
P) Darlene Wright
Q) Barbara Ozen
R) Michael Hayes
S) Martha Sharp
T) Raymond O'Sullivan
U) Carole Klein
V) Ian MacDonald
W) Vincent Eugene Craddock
X) Malcolm John Rebennack
Y) Mark Feld
Z) Paul Gadd

40 Rock All-Sorts

(General; worth 2 points each)

A) **Len Barry** of *1-2-3* and *Like A Baby* fame also led an early sixties' hit recording group. Who were they ?
B) **Richard Perry** formed **Planet Records** in '79, but who also formed a Planet Records in '65 ?
C) Under what name was **T. Rex** originally known ?
D) When did **Rod Stewart** release his first single, what was its title, and on what label ?
E) Two **Berrys** had hits with the same song in '63. Who were they, and what was the song ?
F) Who in '77 was spreading *Rumours* ?
G) How long was **Richard Harris's** *MacArthur Park* single ?
H) In what 1970 movie did the **Alice Cooper** group appear ?
I) What was **Phil Spector's** first top ten hit as a producer ?
J) Who recorded **The Beatles'** *I'll Cry Instead* under the name **Vance Arnold** ?
K) Where is home for **Antonio Carlos Jobim** ?
L) Who used **The Blue Ridge Rangers** as a pseudonym ?
M) What are the full names of **Captain and Tennille** ?
N) Who originally recorded *Needles and Pins* and *When You Walk in the Room* ?
O) What was the name of the **Gibb** brothers' first band ?
P) Who has been called the 'Nabob of Sob', 'Prince of Wails' and 'Cry-Guy' ?
Q) What style of music is associated with New York's CBGB's Club ?
R) Who wrote **Barry Manilow's** massive hit *I Write the Songs* ?
S) Name the film in which **Olivia Newton-John** made her screen debut.
T) Who played Keith Partridge in *The Partridge Family* TV show ?
U) What was the title of the disc **Carole King** released in reply to **Greenfield and Sedaka's** *Oh Carol* tribute ?
V) Who were once known as **The High Numbers** and what was the title of their '64 single release ?
W) Under what name (pre-**Blind Faith**) did **Stevie Winwood** and **Eric Clapton** record together ?
X) What '69 movie used *Everybody's Talkin'* as its main theme, and who composed it ?
Y) Who is known as **'Ole Blue Eyes** ?
Z) Where is the *Mull of Kintyre* ?

Right: The Hondells (*see* 41. N)

41 Summer Means Fun (Surf/hot-rod music)

(Specialist; worth 3 points each)

The Sound of Los Angeles! Since the early sixties, L.A. has been the centre of all that's best in rock music, from the first great musical fad that evolved out of the Californian surf sounds to the supersounds of the late sixties and seventies. A great musical melting-pot of varied tastes, trends and styles . . .

A) By what name were **The Crossfires** later known?
B) In surfing terms, what does **The Chantays'** '63 hit *Pipeline* mean?
C) What pseudonyms did **Phil Sloan and Steve Barri** use on their *Skateboard Craze* single?
D) Who formed the **CT** and **Impact** labels?
E) *Beyond, Space Probe* and *Monsoon* were all minor hits for which Santa Anna group?
F) What was the title of **Gary Usher and The Usherettes'** surf single?
G) Name **Jim Messina's** hot-rod group.
H) In surfing terms, what does **The Surfaris'** *Wipe-Out* mean?
I) Who produced **The Sunrays'** three big chart entries?
J) Where did **The Astronauts** hail from, what was their big '63 US hit single, and in what '64 **Beach** movie did they make a guest appearance?
K) What Minnesota group scored with *Surfin' Bird*?
L) Who penned the soundtrack to the movie *Skater Dater*?
M) Under what name did KFWB disc jockey **Roger Christian** record *Little Street Machine* and *Repossession Blues*?
N) After their big chart success with *Little Honda,* what **Brian Wilson** song did **The Hondells** release as a follow-up?
O) Name the individuals who were **The Tradewinds** of *New York's A Lonely Town* (*When You're the Only Surfer Boy*) fame.
P) What **Beach Boy** song did **Jan and Dean** transform into *Sidewalk Surfin'*?
Q) How were **The Pyramids** distinguishable from other groups?
R) Who was the featured vocalist on many of **The Super Stocks'** recordings?
S) What group originally surfed *Miserlou*?
T) Where did **Ronny and The Daytonas** (of *GTO, California Bound, Beach Boy* and *Sandy* fame) hail from?
U) Who were the masterminds behind **The Rip Chords'** big chart success?
V) Under what title was **The Legendary Masked Surfers'** *Gonna Hustle You* first released?
W) What record label became tagged 'The Originators of Surf Music'?
X) Who supplied the soundtrack to **Bruce Brown's** surf feature, *The Endless Summer*?

Y) What group shared backing tracks with **Jan and Dean** ?
Z) By what name were **The Lively Ones** originally known ?

42 Starfile/Jan and Dean

(Specialist; worth 3 points each)

A) What are **Jan and Dean's** full names ?
B) On which record label was *Jennie Lee* released ?
C) Who penned their *There's A Girl* single ?
D) Where were the original tracks of their early hits recorded ?
E) Who produced the '62 *Tennessee* hit ?
F) Name the two **Brian Wilson** songs that appeared on the album *Jan and Dean Take Linda Surfin'*.
G) What was the title of their '63 US number one hit single ?
H) Name the duo's '64 hit single released between *Ride The Wild Surf* and *Sidewalk Surfin'*.
I) What **Jan and Dean** car song was covered by **The Who** ?
J) Where and when was **Jan's** near-fatal automobile accident ?

Below: Brian Wilson (see 43. B & D)

43 Beach Boys' Music

(Specialist; worth 3 points each)

A) In *I Get Around* who knows them but leaves them alone ?

B) What was the single from **Pet Sounds** credited to **Brian Wilson** alone ?

C) World land speed record-holder **Craig Breedlove** is the subject of a song. Name the song and the album on which it originally appeared.

D) Name those who co-wrote these songs with **Brian Wilson:**
1. *Little Deuce Coupe*
2. *In My Room*
3. *Fun, Fun, Fun*
4. *God Only Knows*
5. *Surfs Up*
6. *Ding Dang*

E) What famous author and novel are mentioned in the lyrics of *California Saga*, and who wrote them ?

44 Mystery Openers

(General; worth 2 points each)

Give the titles of the opening tracks on the following albums:

A) **The Byrds'** *Sweetheart of the Rodeo* ('68)
B) **Alice Coopers'** *Welcome To My Nightmare* ('75)
C) **Badfinger's** *Straight Up* ('72)
D) **Spirit's** *The Family That Plays Together* ('69)
E) **The Four Seasons'** *Helicon* ('77)
F) **Ace Cannon's** *That Music City Feeling* ('74)
G) **Nancy Sinatra's** *Boots* ('66)
H) **Joni Mitchell's** *Ladies of the Canyon* ('70)
I) **Stevie Wonder's** *Songs In the Key of Life* ('76)
J) **Andrew Gold's** *All This and Heaven Too* ('78)
K) **Wings'** *Red Rose Speedway* ('73)
L) **Mary Wells'** *My Guy* ('64)
M) **Electric Light Orchestra's** *Out of the Blue* ('77)
N) **Carly Simon's** *Playing Possum* ('76)
O) **Talking Heads'** *More Songs About Buildings and Food* ('78)
P) **Charlie Byrd and Cal Tjader's** *Tambu* ('74)
Q) **Don Williams'** *Volume Two* ('74)
R) **Chic's** *Chic* ('78)
S) **Thelma Houston's** *Anyway You Like It* ('76)
T) **America's** *Holiday* ('74)
U) **Jose Feliciano's** *Feliciano !* ('68)
V) **The Surfaris'** *Fun City USA* ('64)
W) **Warren Zevon's** *Excitable Boy* ('78)
X) **Steve Cropper's** *With a Little Help From My Friends* ('69)
Y) **Elvis Presley's** *On Stage* ('70)
Z) **George Harrison's** *George Harrison* ('79)

45 Starfile/The Surfaris

(Specialist; worth 3 points each)

A) Where did the group hail from?
B) Name the original line-up.
C) *Surfer Joe*, the B-side of *Wipe Out*, became a hit in its own right. Who penned it?
D) Who was responsible for the hyena-inspired laugh on their *Wipe Out*, *Tequila* and *Point Panic* records?
E) Owing to contractual problems, their American Decca re-makes of *Wipe Out* and *Surfer Joe* were not included on the UK version of *The Surfaris Play* album. What tracks took their place?
F) Over which auto-movie did they sing *Boss Barracuda*?
G) Who produced their *Don't Hurt My Little Sister* single?
H) Give the title of their folk-rock album.
I) Who replaced **Pat Connolly** after his departure from the group?
J) Name their mid-sixties single produced by **J.J. Cale.**

46 Rock All-Sorts

(General; worth 2 points each)

A) What was the name of the drummer who filled in for **Ringo** on **The Beatles'** '64 Dutch, Danish and Far Eastern tour?
B) Who were the first group to use a fuzz box?
C) What was the title of **Blue Cheer's** '68 debut album?
D) What was the name of *The Leader of The Pack*?
E) Name the original **Righteous Brothers.**
F) What do country star **Dave 'Stringbean' Akeman** and **M.G. Al Jackson** have in common?
G) Who is **Dionne Warwick's** singing sister?
H) Why did **Godley and Creme** leave **10 c.c.** in '76?
I) On what **Dusty Springfield** album was the song *Son of a Preacher Man* originally featured?
J) Who was described by writer **Tom Wolfe** as 'the first tycoon of teen'?
K) Who directed **Sonny and Cher's** *Good Times* movie?
L) What was the title of **Carole Bayer Sager's** '77 UK hit single?
M) Who penned and sang the title song to **Neil Simon's** movie *The Goodbye Girl*?
N) Name the boxer who recorded **Paul Simon's** *The Boxer*.

Left: Canned Heat (*see* 46. O)

O) Which member of **Canned Heat** was nicknamed **The Bear**?

P) How many eyes did *The Purple People Eater* have, and who sang about it?

Q) Who penned **Manfred Mann's Earth Band's** '76 *Blinded By The Light* hit single?

R) What band was *Waiting for Columbus*?

S) Where did **Deaf School** form?

T) Who was dubbed 'the Jesus of Cool'?

U) What was the title of **Scott Walker's** first solo single and who penned it?

V) Who originally recorded *Willie and the Hand Jive*?

W) What part of New York City became tagged **Folk City** in the sixties?

X) Who scored in '69 with *Band of Gold*?

Y) In what **Nicholas Roeg** movie did **David Bowie** head the cast?

Z) Who was the inspiration behind **Steve Stills'** *Suite: Judy Blue Eyes*?

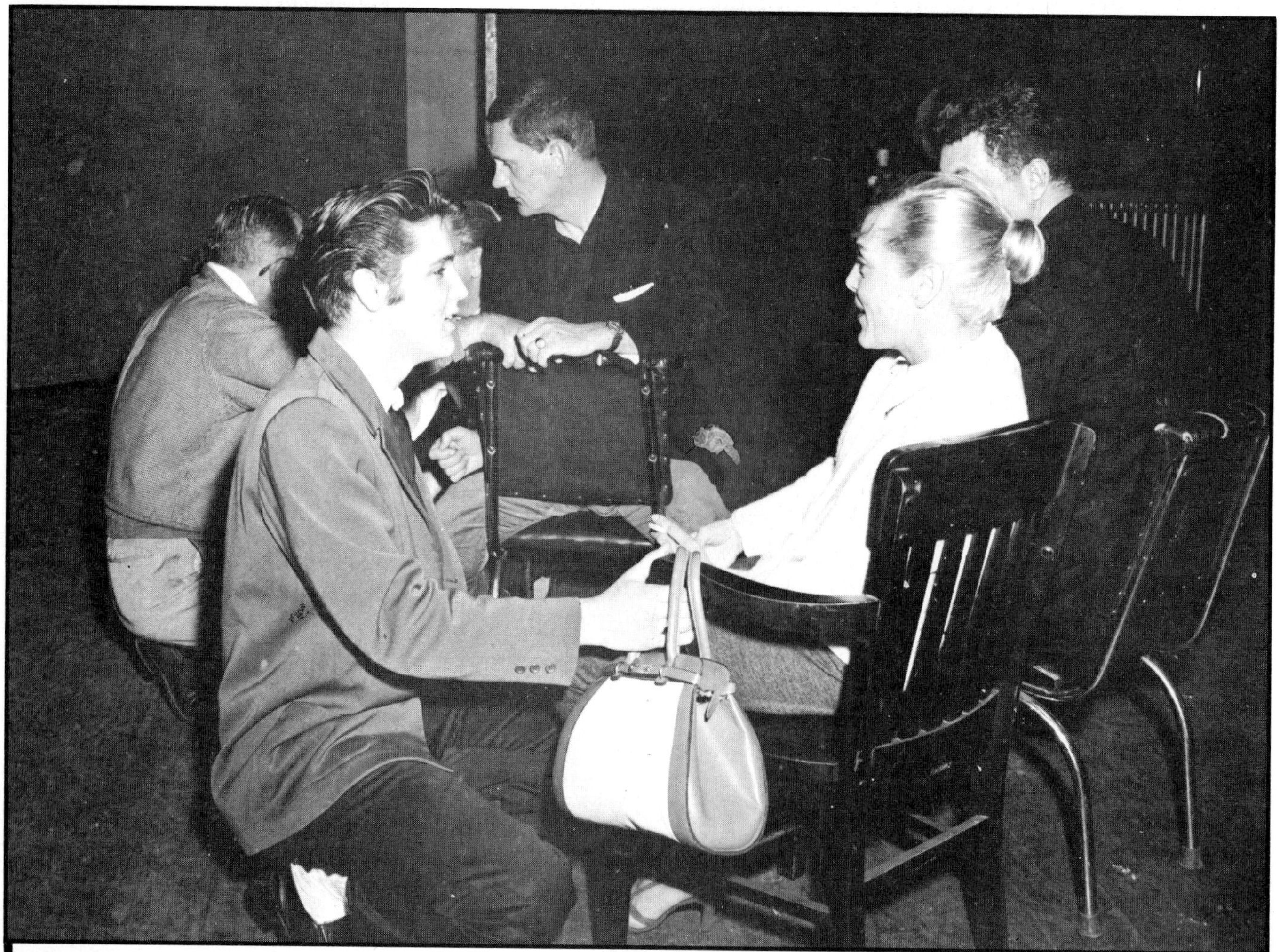

Celluloid Rock 4

(Specialist; worth 3 points each)

A) Who are the stars (left to right) relaxing between takes?

B) Name the movie.

C) Who directed the film?

D) What year was it released?

E) What was the name of the character portrayed by the actor pictured in the foreground?

F) Which record company released the soundtrack?

47 Starfile/The Byrds

(Specialist; worth 3 points each)

A) Under what name did they release *Please Let Me Love You* in '64 ?

B) Name the original line-up.

C) Who produced their **Columbia** debut album, and what was its title ?

D) Which member departed after the *Turn, Turn, Turn* album ?

E) In the summer of '65 they became regular attractions at two LA clubs. What were their names ?

F) With what kind of guitar has **Jim McGuinn** become associated ?

G) Who produced the album that **Crosby** left half-way complete, and what was its title ?

H) Where did the sleeve design of *Sweetheart of the Rodeo* originate ?

I) **Gram Parsons** joined in '68. What was the name of his previous group ?

J) What year was the original **Byrds'** reunion album released ?

Right: Harper's Bizarre (*see* 48. H, O & V)

48 L.A. Rock

(Specialist; worth 3 points each)

A) Where and when was **Terry Melcher** and **Bruce Johnston's** only live engagement as the duo **Bruce and Terry**?
B) Under what name were **Love** originally known, who formed the group, and which ex-member of **The Surfaris** played bass?
C) What were Cheetah, Kaleidoscope, Rendezvous and Shrine Exposition?

D) Name the original **Buffalo Springfield** line-up.
E) Who were **The Jet Set**?
F) What was the title of **Sonny and Cher's** joint US/UK '65 number one hit single?
G) Where was **Jim Morrison** arrested for alleged indecent exposure on stage?
H) Under what name were **Harper's Bizarre** originally known?
I) What was the title of **Barry McGuire's** follow-up single after his monster *Eve of Destruction* hit?
J) Where was the bank at which **Harry Nilsson** was employed?
K) Who penned *For What It's Worth* as a response to the clashes between teenagers and police on Sunset Strip in '66?
L) In which two influential West Coast groups has Canadian-born **Alexander 'Skip' Spence** played. 1. drums and 2. guitar?
M) When was **Joni Mitchell's** *Big Yellow Taxi* a major UK hit single and from what album was it taken?
N) What member of **Spirit** sported a shaved head?
O) Who penned **Harper's Bizarre's** *Come to the Sunshine*?
P) **The Electric Flag** were heard on the soundtrack of which **Peter Fonda/Dennis Hopper** movie?
Q) What was the title of **The Doors'** post-Morrison album?
R) What were *Shindig* and *Hullabaloo*?
S) Who formed **Dunhill** and **Ode Records**?
T) Give the title of **The Mamas and Papas'** autobiographical hit single.
U) How long was **Love's** *Revelation*, cut from their *Da Capo* album?
V) Name the title song **Harper's Bizarre** sang over a **Peter Sellers'** movie.
W) Name the other three musicians heard on the **Bloomfield/Kooper/Stills** '68 *Super Session* album.
X) Who produced **The Peanut Butter Conspiracy's** *Great Conspiracy* album?
Y) Name the group who recorded a one-off album that featured such songs as *I Won't Leave My Wooden Wife For You, Sugar* and *The American Way of Love* (3 parts).
Z) Give the title of **The Mothers of Invention's** debut album.

49 Starfile/The Doors

(Specialist; worth 3 points each)

A) Name the individual line-up.
B) Which members were once in **The Psychedelic Rangers'** band?
C) Where did *Alabama Song,* featured on their debut *Doors* album, originate?
D) Give the title of their debut single.
E) Who played bass on the *Waiting for the Sun* album?
F) Name their US number one hit single that closely resembled **The Kinks'** *All Day and All of the Night.*
G) Where was **Morrison** arrested for using obscene language and starting a riot?
H) From what album was the *Riders On The Storm* single culled?
I) Where and when did **Morrison** mysteriously die of a heart attack?
J) What was the title of **The Doors'** '78 album of **Morrison's** poems set to music?

50 Rock Duos

(General; worth 2 points each)

Pair off the following:

A) **Peaches and**
B) **Delaney and**
C) **Jan and**
D) **Paul and**
E) **Sonny and**
F) **Jet and**
G) **Nancy and**
H) **Sam and**
I) **Fame and**
J) **Bob and**
K) **Captain and**
L) **Dave and**
M) **Dale and**
N) **Dick and**
O) **Santo and**
P) **Donny and**
Q) **Flatt and**
R) **Inez and**
S) **David and**
T) **Gallagher and**
U) **Chad and**
V) **Shirley and**
W) **Ashford and**
X) **Mac and**
Y) **Ike and**
Z) **Simon and**

51 Starfile/The Mamas and Papas

(Specialist; worth 3 points each)

A) Where did **The Mamas and Papas** form ?
B) Who introduced them to producer **Lou Adler** ?
C) Give the titles of their debut single and album.
D) Name the '67 rock festival in which they played a big part.
E) Which member penned and co-produced **Scott McKenzie's** San Francisco hippie anthem ?
F) Who scored with the *California Earthquake* solo outing ?
G) Give the title of their '71 reunion album.
H) Name the 1970 **Robert Altman** movie which **John Phillips** produced.
I) In which **Ken Russell** movie did **Michelle** star ?
J) Where and when did **Cass Elliot** die ?

52 Rock All-Sorts

(General; worth 2 points each)

A) What was the title of **Generation X's** debut single?

B) Who produced **Mink**

DeVille's '78 *Return to Magenta* album?

C) Name the group which features **Martina Weymouth** on bass.

D) Who scored in '69 with *Color Him Father*?

E) Who portrayed two pop singers in the *My Teenage Idol Is Missing* episode of *The New Adventures of Wonder Woman* TV series?

F) What was the title of **Abba's** entry into the '73 *Eurovision Song Contest* stakes?

G) Which new-wave group supported **Marc Bolan** on his last tour?

H) Where is **David Bowie** on the sleeve of *The Rise and*

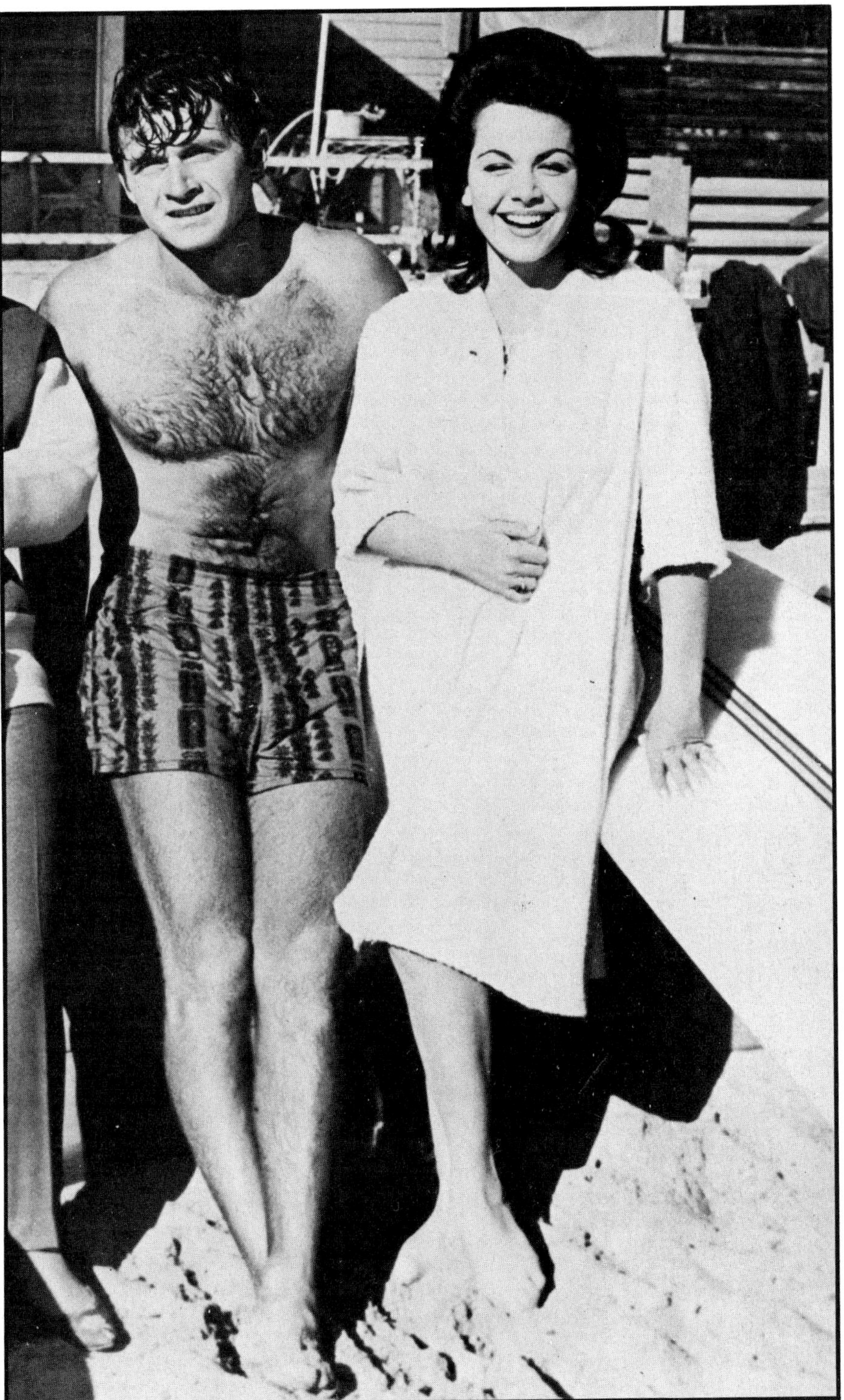

Picture Quiz 5

(Specialist; worth 3 points each)

A) Identify this guitarist pictured in '64 with **Annette Funicello.**

B) Finish these two titles by which he is known:
1. King of the ....
2. The Pied Piper of ......

C) Name his backing group.

D) What was the title of his biggest hit, covered by many groups including **The Beach Boys**?

E) Where was he born?

F) What '73 Hollywood Palladium show did he headline?

G) Name his '62 debut album.

Below: **Cliff Richard and The Shadows** (*see* 52. O)

Fall of Ziggy Stardust and The Spiders from Mars album?

I) Who sings with **The Coral Reefer Band**?

J) Name the group who in '73 released an orchestrated reworking of **Chuck Berry's** *Roll Over Beethoven.*

K) Give the surname of **Fanny's Jean** and **June.**

L) Who sang a duet with actress **Susan George** on a '73 version of *We've Only Just Begun*?

M) What was **Linda Eastman's** full time occupation before becoming a musician?

N) Who scored the soundtrack of the '66 movie *Alfie*?

O) Where was **Cliff Richard and The Shadows'** March 4 1978 (*Thank You Very Much*) reunion concert held?

P) What style of music can be heard on the '78 **Rhino** various artists *Saturday Night Pogo* album?

Q) Who scored with the *New Boots and Panties* album?

R) Name the group who made the singles charts in 1970 with *Black Skin Blue Eyed Boys.*

S) With what songwriting partnership did **Dionne Warwick** enjoy great chart success during the sixties?

T) What South African instrumental group scored in '58 with the *Tom Hark* single?

U) In what '68 movie was **Noel Harrison's** *Windmills of Your Mind* the main theme?

V) What instruments did the girls in the following groups play? 1. **The Honeycombs;** 2. **The Applejacks.**

W) Who made it to the UK number one single spot in '64 with *Yeh Yeh*?

X) Where did **The Cars** hail from?

Y) Who supplied a cameo vocal shout of '1 2 3' on **The Dictators'** *Bloodbrothers* album?

Z) Who has been dubbed **The Divine Miss M**?

53 Starfile/Nilsson
(Specialist; worth 3 points each)

A) Give **Nilsson's** full name.
B) Under what name did he record *Donna* on the Mercury label?
C) Who recorded his song, *Cuddly Toy*?
D) What was the title of his **RCA** debut album?
E) Name the TV series in which he made his acting debut.
F) What was the title of the song he penned for the movie *Midnight Cowboy* which was rejected in preference to his version of *Everybody's Talkin'*?
G) Name one of the two songs he has recorded which was penned by his mother.
H) What was his role in the film *Skidoo*?
I) Name the producers of these albums:
1. *Harry*
2. *Nilsson Schmilsson*
3. *A Touch of Schmilsson*
4. *Pussycats*
J) What is the title of his musical fairytale?

54 Rock All-Sorts

(General; worth 2 points each)

A) Which **Monkee,** surrounded by a hail of publicity, met **Paul McCartney** in London in February '68 ?

B) Where did **Tony Bennett** leave his heart in '62 ?

C) Under what name is **Chester Arthur Burnett** better known ?

D) What was the title of **David and Jonathan's** self-penned '66 hit single ?

E) Who has been called a 'bargain-basement' **Pete Seeger** ?

F) On what '69 single were **Tommy Smothers, Dr. Timothy Leary, Derek Taylor** and a Rabbi featured as part of the line-up ?

G) Give the title of **Tom Jones's** debut disc.

H) Who recorded the original version of *Do You Wanna Dance* ?

I) What ex-member of **The United States of America** produced **Ry Cooder's** '78 *Jazz* album ?

J) Where were the famed **Fillmore Theaters,** and who was their director ?

K) Who led the **Dawn** trio ?

L) Name the six guest celebrities on the sleeve pic of **Wings'** *Band on The Run* album.

M) Who performed the title song of **Stanley Kramer's** '71 movie *Bless the Beasts and Children* ?

N) Give the title of **Ace**

Celluloid Rock 5

(Specialist; worth 3 points each)

A) Name the movie.

B) Who is pictured in this still on stage rehearsing the opening scene ?

C) What year was the film released ?

D) Who directed it ?

E) Which record company released the title song from the soundtrack ?

Cannon's big '61 hit single.

O) Who founded **Atlantic Records**?

P) With what song did **Abba** win the '74 Eurovision Song Contest?

Q) Who in '77 were *Livin' On The Fault Line*?

R) Give the surname of **Danny** of **Danny and The Juniors.**

S) Give the title of **Elvis Costello's** third album.

T) Who did **Jimmy Gilmer** sing with?

U) Name one of **Dion's Belmonts.**

V) Give the title of **Todd Rundgren's** '76 album, on which side one is wall-to-wall recreations of other group's hits.

W) What was the title of **The**

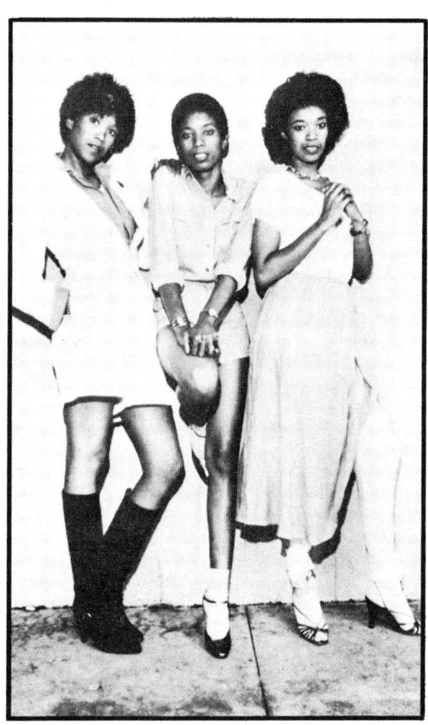

Pointer Sisters' debut single on **Planet Records**?

X) Who co-penned *You Belong To Me* with **Carly Simon**?

Y) Where were the **Bay City Rollers** from, and under what name were they originally known?

Z) Who scored in '68 with *The Son of Hickory Holler's Tramp*?

Picture Quiz 6

(Specialist; worth 3 points each)

A) Identify this musician.

B) Name his self-penned bass guitar showcase featured on **The Shadows'** debut album.

C) When (full date) did he depart from **The Shadows**?

D) What was the title of his first vocal solo disc and the date of release?

E) As one half of a duo he scored with a trio of UK top ten singles in '63. Name the third hit and his partner on it.

F) In which '63 movie did the duo make a guest appearance?

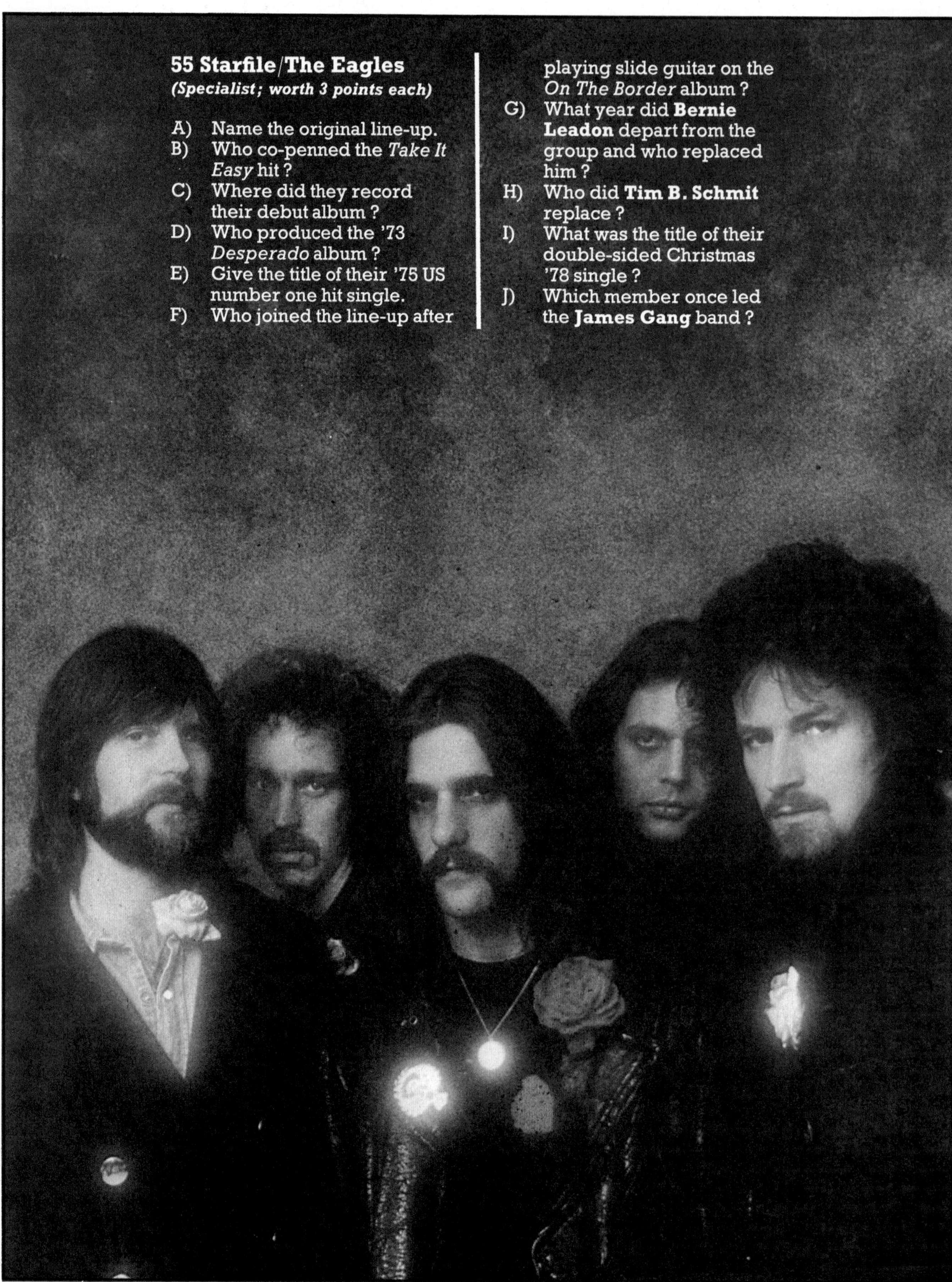

55 Starfile/The Eagles

(Specialist; worth 3 points each)

A) Name the original line-up.
B) Who co-penned the *Take It Easy* hit ?
C) Where did they record their debut album ?
D) Who produced the '73 *Desperado* album ?
E) Give the title of their '75 US number one hit single.
F) Who joined the line-up after playing slide guitar on the *On The Border* album ?
G) What year did **Bernie Leadon** depart from the group and who replaced him ?
H) Who did **Tim B. Schmit** replace ?
I) What was the title of their double-sided Christmas '78 single ?
J) Which member once led the **James Gang** band ?

56 Superstars/Bob Dylan

(Specialist; worth 3 points each)

From folk poet to living legend, from *Blowin' In The Wind* **to** *Street Legal,* **Bob Dylan has always been, and will always be, a unique musical phenomenon.**

A) What is **Bob Dylan's** real name ?
B) From which poet did he take the name **Dylan** ?
C) When was his debut *Bob Dylan* album released ?
D) At what folk festival did he appear in July '63 ?
E) Who signed him to **Columbia Records** ?
F) In what play did he make his UK TV debut ?
G) On whose '64 US concert tour was he a guest ?
H) Name the traditional songs on which **Dylan** based the following: 1. *Girl From The North Country*; 2. *A Hard*

Rain's Gonna Fall; 3. *Masters of War*.

) Who produced *The Freewheelin' Bob Dylan* album ?

) Name the track and the album on which he made his recording debut playing piano.

K) Who is pictured on the cover of the *Time* magazine which appears on the sleeve photo of *Bringing It All Back Home* ?

L) Which song from *Bringing It All Back Home* was included on the *Easy Rider* movie soundtrack ?

M) Where in July '65 was he booed off stage for appearing with an electric guitar and rock band ?

N) Who directed the documentary movie *Don't Look Back* ?

O) Name the group that took his *Mr Tambourine Man* to the number one singles spot in both the US and UK.

P) What make of motorcycle does he display on the sleeve of *Highway 61 Revisited* ?

Q) Where did he record his first double album, what was its title and the title of the track which took up a whole side ?

R) At whose memorial concert did he make his comeback following a year's absence after a motorcycle accident ?

S) Give the title of his '68 album.

T) How much money was he reported to have earned for a one hour appearance at the **Isle of Wight '69 Festival** ?

U) Who was asked if it was rollin' on the *Nashville Skyline* album ?

V) Which group became his backing band ?

W) Where did he appear in August '71 ?

X) Give the title of his first novel.

Y) Name the '73 **Sam Peckinpah** movie in which he appeared.

Z) What is the title of the opening track on his '78 *Street Legal* album ?

Celluloid Rock 6

(Specialist; worth 3 points each)

A) Name the movie.

B) Who played the character Jim Stark ?

C) What location is pictured in this behind-the-scenes shot ?

D) Which character in the movie met his death at this location ?

E) Who directed the film ?

F) Who composed the soundtrack ?

Right: Alice Cooper (see 57. P)

57 Rock All-Sorts

(General; worth 2 points each)

A) **Robin Sarstedt's** two brothers have both separately scored UK number one hit singles. What are their names and the titles of their major hits ?

B) Who has sometimes been credited as **Dr Winston O'Boogie** ?

C) Name the Jamacian group who scored in '65 with *Guns of Navarone.*

D) Who was **Love Affair's** lead singer ?

E) Was it **Jay and The Americans** or **Jay and The Techniques** who scored in '67 with *Apples, Peaches, Pumpkin Pie* ?

F) Who penned the instrumental *Angie* (recorded by **Simon and Garfunkel, Bert Jansch** and others) ?

G) What was the title of **Jam's** debut album ?

H) Who originally recorded *Walk Away Renee* ?

I) What singer/songwriter played a part in the **Robert Redford/Marlon Brando** movie *The Chase* ?

J) Who portrayed the group **Flame** in the '75 movie of the same name ?

K) What group scored in the sixties with this trio of hits : *The Letter* ('67), *Cry Like A Baby* ('68), and *Soul Deep* ('69) ?

L) Who is **Lynsey Rubin** better known as ?

M) On what label did **Mike Oldfield** release *Tubular Bells* ?

N) **Bram Tchaikovsky** departed from what group to follow a solo career ?

O) Who in '79 released a hit version of the old **Rodgers and Hart** standard *My Funny Valentine* ?

P) What was the title of the album inspired by **Alice Cooper's** bout of alcoholism ?

Q) Name **Ray Campi's** backing group.

R) Who wrote the original stage production of *Grease* ?

S) Give the title of **Bobby Goldsboro's** big '68 hit single.

T) What instrument do you associate with **Al Hirt** ?

U) Who scored in '59 with *Tallahassie Lassie* ?

V) What was the title of **Jane Birkin and Serge Gainsbourg's** '69 heavy breather ?

W) Who's the Billy of *Billy's Bag* ?

X) Under what name did **The Rondells** become better known ?

Y) What year did **Bobby Vinton** score with *Roses Are Red (My Love)* ?

Z) Who penned **The Foundations'** '68 hit single *Build Me Up, Buttercup* ?

58 Dylan Music

(Specialist; worth 3 points each)

A) Where was Johnny in *Subterranean Homesick Blues* ?

B) What is the title of the **Paul Simon** song included on his *Self-portrait* album ?

C) In *Just Like A Woman,* what does she break like ?

D) Who took these **Dylan** songs into the singles charts ?
 1. *Too Much of Nothing*
 2. *If You Gotta Go, Go Now*
 3. *This Wheel's On Fire*
 4. *You Ain't Goin' Nowhere*
 5. *All Along the Watchtower*

E) What does Maggie's Ma talk to the servants about in *Maggie's Farm* ?

F) What was the hit title theme from **Dylan's Sam Peckinpah** movie ?

G) Name the four tracks which were included on early copies of *The Freewheelin'* album, but not on later copies.

H) Who backed him on the *Concert for Bangla Desh* album ?

I) What was on the B-side of **The Band's** US *The Weight* single ?

J) Give the title of the song included on **George Harrison's** *All Things Must Pass* set that he co-penned with **Harrison.**

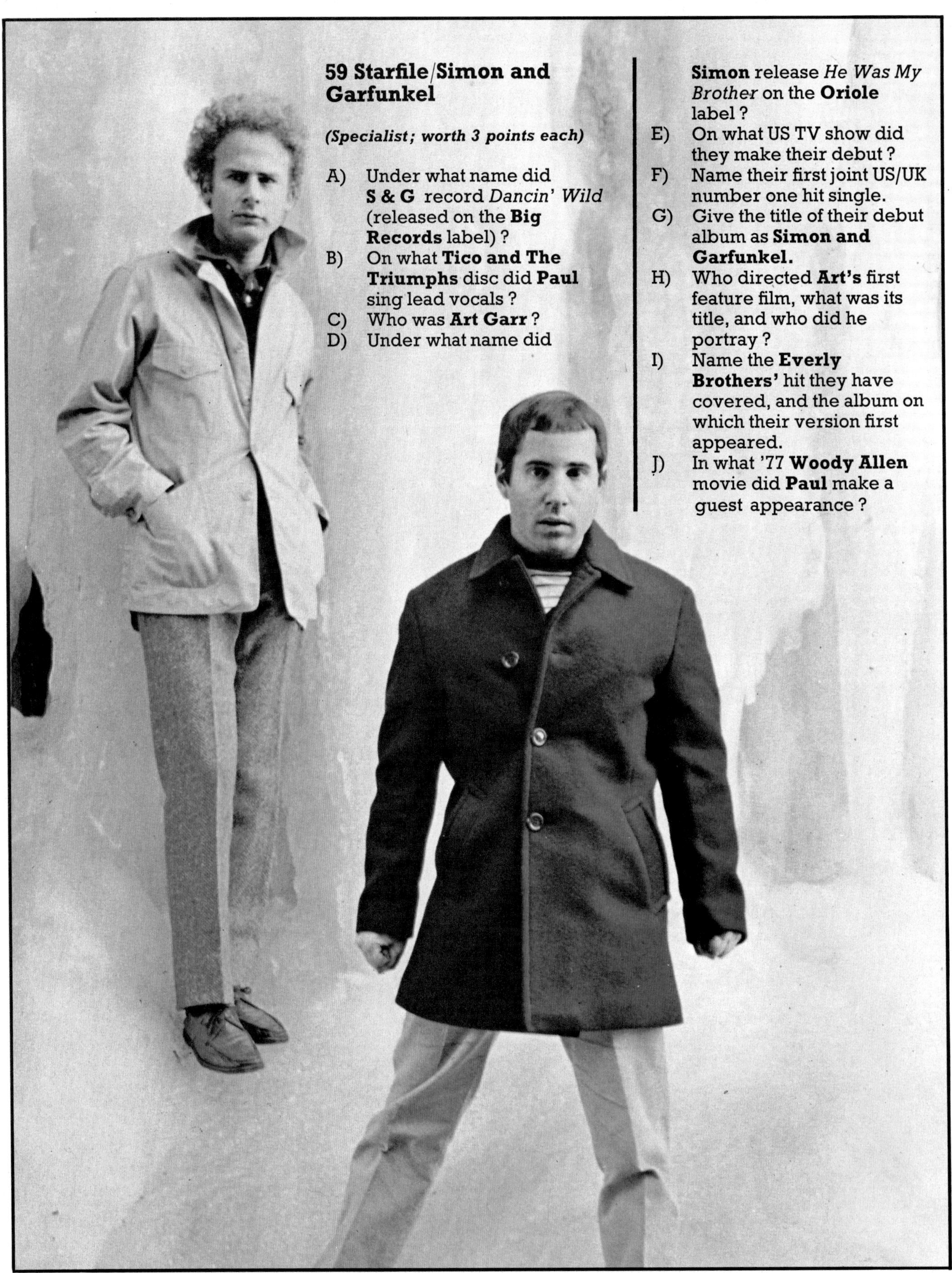

59 Starfile/Simon and Garfunkel

(Specialist; worth 3 points each)

A) Under what name did **S & G** record *Dancin' Wild* (released on the **Big Records** label)?
B) On what **Tico and The Triumphs** disc did **Paul** sing lead vocals?
C) Who was **Art Garr**?
D) Under what name did **Simon** release *He Was My Brother* on the **Oriole** label?
E) On what US TV show did they make their debut?
F) Name their first joint US/UK number one hit single.
G) Give the title of their debut album as **Simon and Garfunkel.**
H) Who directed **Art's** first feature film, what was its title, and who did he portray?
I) Name the **Everly Brothers'** hit they have covered, and the album on which their version first appeared.
J) In what '77 **Woody Allen** movie did **Paul** make a guest appearance?

60 Starfile/The Band

(Specialist; worth 3 points each)

A) Where did they form?
B) Under what name were they originally known, and who was their first front man?
C) Name the individual members.
D) When did they start their working relationship with **Dylan**?
E) What was the title of their debut album, and who illustrated its sleeve?
F) Name the track and the studio album on which they were joined by **Van Morrison** on vocals.
G) Give the title of their 1970 UK hit single.
H) Name the album that featured old rock numbers such as *The Great Pretender* and *Mystery Train*.
I) What was **The Band's** '76 farewell concert dubbed?
J) Which member produced **Neil Diamond's** *Beautiful Noise* album?

61 Folk Music

(Specialist; worth 3 points each)

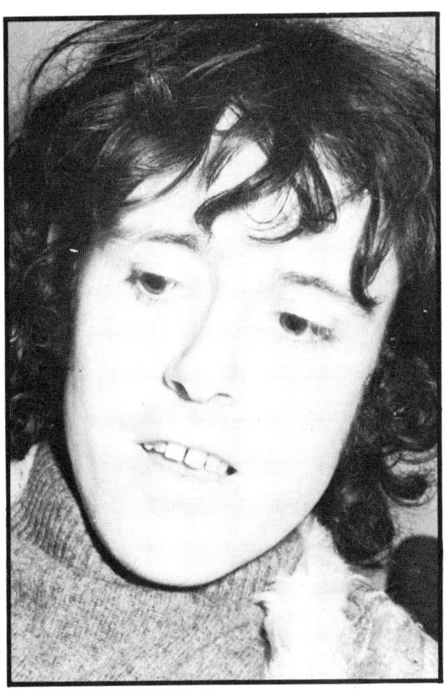

Above: Donovan (*see* 61. G)

A) What is the full title of **Paul Simon's** *Feelin' Groovy*?
B) Who recorded in '63 under the pseudonym **Blindboy Grunt**?
C) Give **Woody Guthrie's** full name.
D) Who penned **The Kingston Trio's** '63 *Greenback Dollar* hit?
E) Where were the Third Side, Gaslight and Playhouse coffee houses?
F) Who wrote the original poem that became **Pete Seeger's** *Bells of Rhymney*?
G) What was the title of **Donovan's** debut single?
H) Who scored in '63 with **Dylan's** *Blowin' in the Wind*?
I) What was the title of **Richard Farina's** novel, and who was his famous sister-in-law?
J) Who starred in the '69 movie of his self-penned song, and what was its title?

Above: Woody Guthrie (*see* 61. C)

62 Starfile/Joan Baez

(Specialist; worth 3 points each)

A) With whom in '59 did **Joan** record for the very first time?
B) When was her solo debut album released?
C) In what year did she appear on the cover of *Time* magazine?
D) Name the institute she helped form at Carmel Valley in '65.
E) Who produced her '66 never-to-be-released rock album?
F) Why was her then husband, **David Harris,** sent to prison in '68?
G) Give the UK title of her 1970 movie.
H) Name her singer/song-writer sister.
I) What was the title of her 1970 autobiography?
J) Whose *Rolling Thunder* tour did she join in '75?

Celluloid Rock 7

(Specialist; worth 3 points each)

A) Name the movie.
B) Who was its director?
C) Identify the two stars pictured here and give the names of the characters they portrayed.
D) In what decade was the film set?
E) Who portrayed **The Hurricanes'** drummer?
F) Whose hit single gave the movie its title?

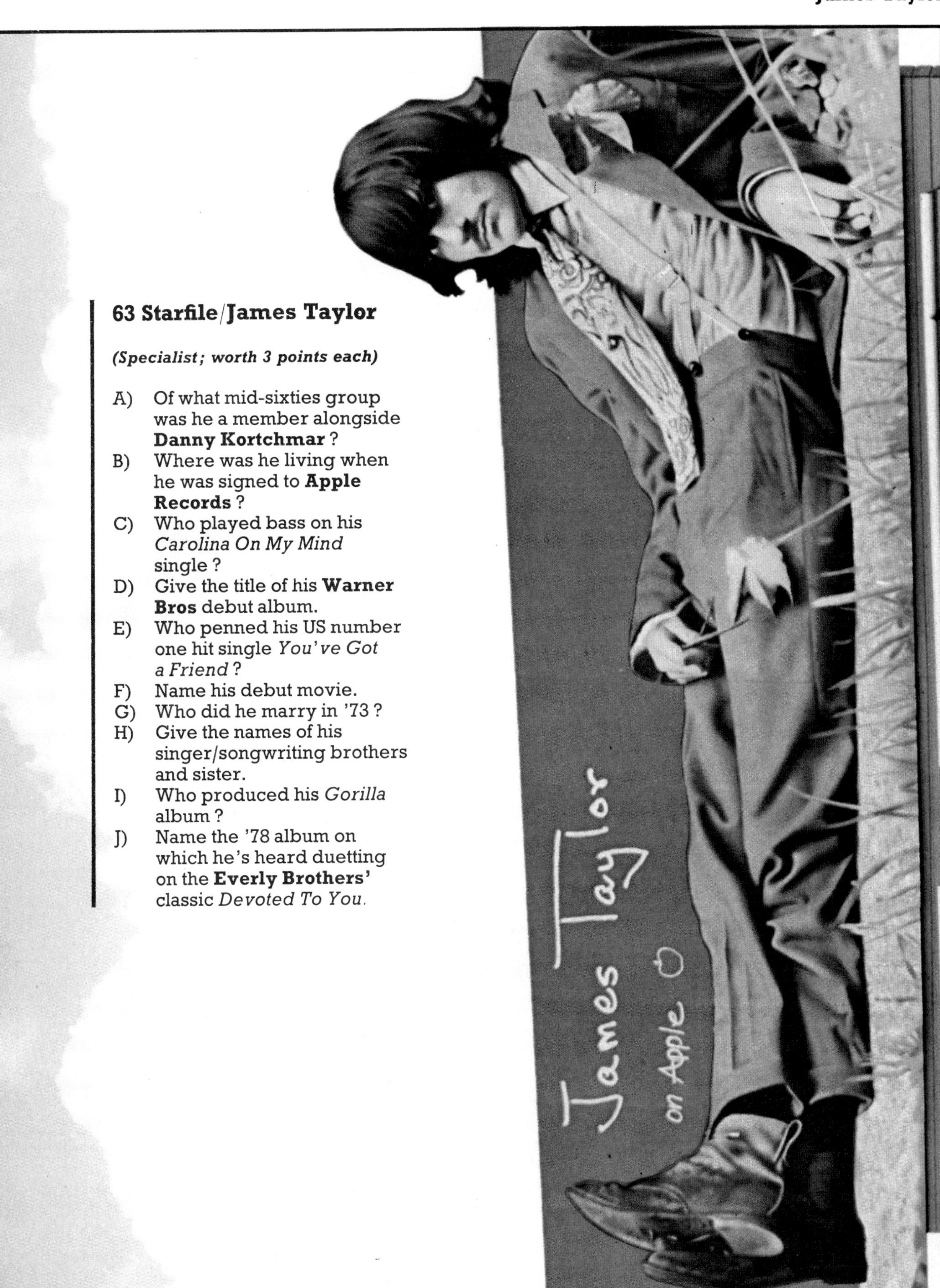

63 Starfile/James Taylor

(Specialist; worth 3 points each)

A) Of what mid-sixties group was he a member alongside **Danny Kortchmar** ?
B) Where was he living when he was signed to **Apple Records** ?
C) Who played bass on his *Carolina On My Mind* single ?
D) Give the title of his **Warner Bros** debut album.
E) Who penned his US number one hit single *You've Got a Friend* ?
F) Name his debut movie.
G) Who did he marry in '73 ?
H) Give the names of his singer/songwriting brothers and sister.
I) Who produced his *Gorilla* album ?
J) Name the '78 album on which he's heard duetting on the **Everly Brothers'** classic *Devoted To You*.

Below: Jefferson Airplane (*see* 64. J, M & O)

64 The Love Crowd

(Specialist; worth 3 points each)

Frisco's music bloomed in the flowerpower summer of '67, ablaze with psychedelic colours, hippie gatherings and the sounds of acid rock, establishing San Francisco as a major rock music city.

A) Who fronted **The Great Society**?
B) Which pop-artist became famous for his **Avalon Ballroom** posters, *Surfer* magazine's *Murf the Surf* and **The Grateful Dead** album sleeves, among other works?
C) Who organized the *A Tribute to Doctor Strange* dance/concert held on October 16, 1965?
D) Name the group who released the '69 *Happy Trails* album.
E) By what name did **The Warlocks** become better known?
F) What were *The Holy See, Pacific Grass and Electric, Head Lights* and *North American Ibex Alchemical Co*?
G) Who introduced us to *The Fish Cheer*?
H) What mid-sixties group did **Janis Joplin** front?
I) Who was dubbed **The Space Cowboy**?
J) Give the titles of **Jefferson Airplane's** two '67 hit singles.

K) Where were the **Sir Douglas Quintet** formed ?

L) What DJ became **Dino Valenti's** manager and formed the **North Beach** label ?

M) **Jefferson Airplane** changed their name to what ?

N) Under what title was the **Eddie Cochran** song *Blue Cheer* revamped ?

O) Why did **Signe Anderson** leave **Jefferson Airplane** ?

P) Who were once known as **Mother Macree's Uptown Jug Champions** ?

Picture Quiz 7

(Specialist; worth 3 points each)

A) Identify the couple pictured
B) What Doll did he sing about in '58?
C) She sang the title song of her daddy's '67 movie. Name the movie.
D) He sang a duet over the title of a **Hayley Mills** movie. With whom did he sing, and what was the title of the song?
E) In which **Presley** movie did she appear?
F) In what '61 film did he co-star with **Fabian**?

Q) What group formed the **Grunt** label?
R) Who released the *Wow* album in '68?
S) Which group featured **David LaFlamme** on violin?
T) Name the group who started a chain of hit singles with a re-working of **Dale Hawkins'** *Suzie Q*
U) Give the profession of **Victor Moscoso, Wes Wilson, Stanley Mouse** and **Al Kelley.**
V) Who sang with **The Hot Licks**?
W) What was *The Northern California Psychedelic Cattleman's Association*?
X) When did **Janis Joplin** fatally overdose on heroin?
Y) What two famous names once featured in **The Marksmen Combo**?
Z) Who released the 1970 *American Beauty* album?

65 Rock All-Sorts

(General; worth 2 points each)

A) Where was the **Arts Lab**

that **David Bowie** ran in 1970?
B) By what name is **David Cook** better known?
C) In what movie did **Jayne Mansfield** mime to the voice of **Connie Francis**?
D) Give the title of **Kate Bush's** debut album.
E) Who scored in '64 with *My Boy Lollipop*?
F) Give the title of German singer **Ivo Robic's** international '59 hit single.
G) When everybody was singing about San Francisco, which place were **The Bee Gees** remembering?
H) **Ron Wood** was once a member of a group that were sued by **The Byrds.** What were they called?
I) Name the one-off hit for which **St. Cecilia** were infamous.
J) Who did **Linda Ronstadt** sing with on her early hits?
K) Give the year when *The Pied Piper* was a hit for **Crispian St Peters.**
L) Name the film in which **Jimmy Rodgers** made his screen debut.
M) Name the two movie title songs which achieved chart success for **Gene Pitney** in the early sixties.
N) In what song are **The**

Rolling Stones described as 'Coming from Liverpool'?

O) What famous duo were once members of **The Champs**?

P) **Redbone's Pat** and **Lolly Vegas** were once known as **The Avantis.** Give the title of their single on the **Chancellor** label.

Q) Name the TV series in which **Monkee Mickey Dolenz** appeared as a child actor.

R) Where did the group **Kensington Market** hail from in '68?

S) Who scored in '75 with *Bye Bye, Baby*?

T) Give the title of **The Routers'** hand clapping '62 hit single.

U) Who penned **Barry McGuire's** *Eve of Destruction*?

V) **Zal Yanovsky** of **The Lovin' Spoonful, James Hendrix** of **The Lamp of Childhood** and **Cass Elliot** and **Denny Doherty** of **The Mamas and Papas** once played together in what group?

W) Name the original **Three Dog Night** trio.

X) What group scored in '65 with *Don't Think Twice* under the pseudonym of **Wonder Who**?

Y) The **Bacharach and David** Broadway musical *Promises Promises* was based on what 1960 **Billy Wilder** movie?

Z) Under what name is **Martha Sharp** better known?

Celluloid Rock 8

(Specialist; worth 3 points each)

A) Name three out of the five movies produced in the sixties by American International Pictures under the banner **Beach Movies.**

B) Who directed the series?

C) What year was the original released?

D) Name the leading couple pictured here (front row right).

E) Where were all the films set?

Below: Hank Williams (see 66. R)

66 Country Music

(Specialist; worth 3 points each)

One of the fastest-growing popular music forms of recent years, Country Music has been aptly described as 'the music of the people, for the people, by the people'.

A) Name **Roy Acuff's** first Hillbilly band.

B) Give the title of **Johnny Cash and June Carter's** 1970 cross-over hit single.

C) Who is affectionately known as **Pig**?

D) What Californian town has been tagged **Nashville West**?

E) Who is heard over the TV series *The Dukes of Hazzard*?

F) Give the title of the **Flatt and Scruggs** theme heard on the *Bonnie and Clyde* movie soundtrack.

G) Name **Jessi Colter's** first husband.

H) With what instrument do you associate **Lloyd Green**?

I) Name the individual **Blue Sky Boys.**

J) Give the title of **Jim Reeve's** one and only movie.

K) Who is known as **Peter Nolan** in TV's *Rawhide* series, and as **Ben Colder** on comedy discs?

L) What was the title of **Dolly Parton's** '76 international hit single?

M) Who joined **Waylon Jennings** on the '76 *Outlaws* album?

N) Who originated the **Dobro** guitar?

O) With what instrument do you associate **Charlie McCoy**?

P) Under what name is **William Fries** better known?

Q) What was the title of **Tammy Wynette's** '75 UK number one hit single?

R) Who portrayed **Hank Williams** in the bio-pic *Your Cheatin' Heart*?

S) In what oscar-winning Western movie did **Glen Campbell** co-star with **John Wayne**?

T) What renowned guitarist fronted the '73 *Superpickers* album?

U) Who scored with the '63 hit single *The End of the World*?

V) With what instrument do you associate **Floyd Cramer**?

W) Give the title of **Charlie Rich's** big '74 hit single.

X) Who released an album entitled *The Gayest Old Dude In Town*?

Y) Of what group had **Don Williams** been a member prior to turning solo?

Z) Under what name is **Clarence Eugene Snow** better known?

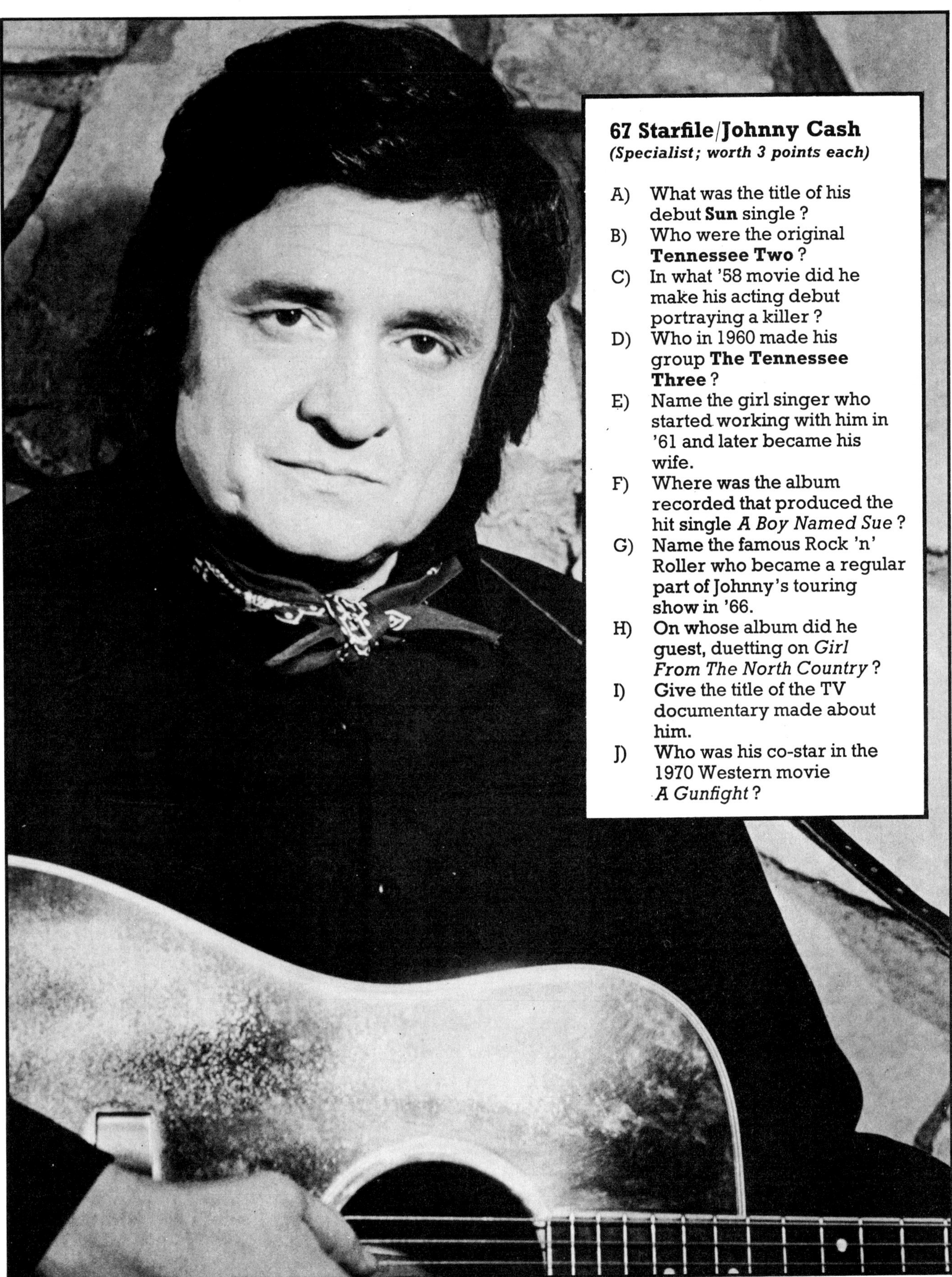

67 Starfile/Johnny Cash

(Specialist; worth 3 points each)

A) What was the title of his debut **Sun** single ?

B) Who were the original **Tennessee Two** ?

C) In what '58 movie did he make his acting debut portraying a killer ?

D) Who in 1960 made his group **The Tennessee Three** ?

E) Name the girl singer who started working with him in '61 and later became his wife.

F) Where was the album recorded that produced the hit single *A Boy Named Sue* ?

G) Name the famous Rock 'n' Roller who became a regular part of Johnny's touring show in '66.

H) On whose album did he guest, duetting on *Girl From The North Country* ?

I) Give the title of the TV documentary made about him.

J) Who was his co-star in the 1970 Western movie *A Gunfight* ?

Left: Marty Robbins (*see* 68. P)

68 Country Music

(Specialist; worth 3 points each)

A) Who scored in '67 with *Skip A Rope*?
B) With what instrument do you associate **Boots Randolph**?
C) Who sang the title song from **Clint Eastwood's** *Every Which Way But Loose* movie?
D) Give the titles of the two **Elvis Presley** hit singles penned by **Jerry Reed.**
E) With what musical style do you associate **Bill Monroe**?
F) Under what name is **Loretta Lynn's** sister, **Brenda Gayle Webb,** better known?
G) Give the year when *Big Bad John* was a big hit for **Jimmy Dean.**
H) Who was tagged 'The Hillbilly Shakespeare'?
I) Where is the *Country Music Hall of Fame* situated?
J) Who penned **Johnny Cash's** *Ring of Fire* hit?
K) Give the title of **Roger Miller's** king-sized '65 hit single.
L) Who has been tagged 'The Nashville Rebel'?
M) With what musical style do you associate **Doug Kershaw**?
N) Name **George Jones'** one-time hit-making wife.
O) Give the title of **Jeannie C. Riley's** '68 US number one hit single.
P) Name two out of the three Western movies in which **Marty Robbins** has appeared.
Q) Who was tagged 'The Kentucky Wonder'?
R) Give the title of the **Dottie West** hit originally heard as a Coke commercial.
S) Who is **Stella's** big sister?
T) With what instrument do you associate **Chet Atkins**?
U) Who produced many of **Don Williams'** best albums and also penned his *I Recall A Gypsy Woman* hit, among others?

Left: Chet Atkins (*see* **68. T**)

V) Name the supergroup comprised of **Nashville** and **Muscle Shoales** sessionmen, among them **Charlie McCoy, Kenneth Buttrey** and **Bobby Thompson.**

W) Over what **Robert Redford** movie did **Johnny Cash** sing **Bob Dylan's** *Wanted Man*?

X) With what instrument do you associate **Vassar Clements**?

Y) Who scored with *Duelling Banjos* from the *Deliverance* movie soundtrack?

Z) Where is the new **Grand Ole Opry** housed?

Celluloid Rock 9

(Specialist; worth 3 points each)

A) Name the movie.

B) Who directed the film?

C) Name the actors pictured in the still.

D) What year was the film released?

69 Starfile/The Carpenters

(Specialist; worth 3 points each)

A) Who played bass in the original **Carpenters'** jazz instrumental trio?
B) In what '66 group competition did they walk away with three awards?
C) Which record company signed them after their '66 competition triumph?
D) Give the name of their '67 vocal group.
E) Who penned their first US number one hit single?
F) Give the original title of their '69 **A&M** *Ticket To Ride* album.
G) Where was *We've Only Just Begun* first heard?
H) Of what US TV show were they the subject in 1970?
I) Who penned their *Superstar* hit single?
J) Give the title of their '73 album which features such oldies as *Our Day Will Come* and *Dead Man's Curve*.

70 Rock All-Sorts

(General; worth 2 points each)

A) Who penned the *Batman* theme, recorded by **The Who, Jan and Dean** and others?

B) Name the US TV series in which **John Maus** of **The Walker Bros** was regularly featured at the age of twelve.

C) Who duetted with **Nancy Sinatra** on 1. *Jackson,*

2. *Somethin' Stupid,* and 3. *Did You Ever?*

D) Where was *Strangers in the Night* first heard?

E) Name the two US record labels under which **The Troggs'** *Wild Thing* was simultaneously released.

F) Under what name were **Gary and The Nite Lights** better known?

G) Give the title of the **Bee Gees'** debut disc.

H) Who scored in '67 with *The Rain, The Park and Other Things?*

I) Name **The Cream** album on which *Sunshine of Your Love* was originally featured.

J) Give the title of **Van Morrison's** first release on

Bang Records.

K) Since the mid-sixties **Eric Stewart** has led three top ten hit singles bands. Name them.

L) Where were **Thin Lizzy** formed?

M) Who penned *By The Time I Get to Pheonix, Up, Up and Away* and *The Yard Went On Forever?*

N) Name the group who scored in both the US and UK with the *Woodstock* single.

O) Give the title of the track on **Frank Zappa's** *Hot Rats* solo album which features

Captain Beefheart on vocals.

P) Under what names did **Caesar and Cleo** become better known?

Q) Name the ex-pop singer who produced some of **James Taylor** and **Linda Ronstadt's** best works.

R) Give the title of **The Rolling Stones'** hit single culled from their *Black and Blue* album.

S) Who sang a duet on the '78 single *Too Much, Too Little, Too Late?*

T) What is **Joni Mitchell's** real name?

U) By what name is **Francis Castelluccio** better known?

V) Where was **Bob Dylan** born?

W) Name the famous duo who came out of **The Turtles** group.

X) Name the original members of **America.**

Y) Who scored in '77 with the *Dancing Queen* hit single?

Z) Give the title of **Elton John's** first movie soundtrack album.

71 Starfile/Pink Floyd

(Specialist; worth 3 points each)

A) What year was the group formed?
B) Name the original line-up.
C) Name the two Georgia bluesmen from whom their name was derived.
D) Give the title of their '67 UK top ten single.
E) Who joined the band in '68 shortly before **Barrett** departed?
F) Give the title of the '69 **Barbet Shroeder** movie for which the group supplied the soundtrack.
G) Where were the **Pink Floyd** shown to be at the '72 Edinburgh Film Festival?
H) Which track was used to great effect in the surf movie *Crystal Voyager*?
I) Give the title of their first US number one album.
J) For whom did they play the December '73 benefit concert?

Picture Quiz 8

(Specialist; worth 3 points each)

A) Identify this group.
B) Which member was once known as **Johnny Volume**?
C) Identify the two members who later joined **The Heartbreakers.**
D) Which member released the *So Alone* album in '78?

72 All That Jazz

(Specialist; worth 3 points each)

Although a major musical form in its own right with many *bona-fide* recordings achieving popular chart success, jazz has also become an indelible influence on the world of rock and pop music.

A) Who gained the nicknames **Pops** and **Satchmo**?

B) What was the full title of **Stan Getz and Charlie Byrd's** big Bossa Nova hit?
C) Who penned **Dave Brubeck's** *Take Five*?
D) What TV theme did **Mr Acker Bilk** take to the number one spot in the US pop charts, and who accompanied him?
E) Name the two **Adderley** brothers.
F) When was the movie *Jazz on a Summer's Day* filmed, and what festival did it document?
G) What was **Jean Reinhardt's** nickname?

Below: The Great Guitars, featuring Bertell Knox (drums) and Joe Byrd (bass) (*see* 72. T)

H) Name the original **Ramsey Lewis** trio of *The 'In Crowd'*,

Hang on Sloopy and *Wade in the Water* fame.

I) In what **Clint Eastwood** movie did an **Erroll Garner** standard play a big part?

J) Where did **Kenny Ball** spend *Midnight*?

K) What instrument is **Jimmy Smith** famous for playing?

L) Who produced **Earl Klugh's** *Magic in Your Eyes* album?

M) Give the title of **Ella Fitzgerald's** first million-seller, and the year in which it was released.

N) Who composed **Wes Montgomery's** *Windy* hit?

O) **Mel Torme** is known as a 'Cool School' vocalist. What was his big **Ben Tucker/Bob Dorough**-penned hit?

P) What was **Chick Corea's** *Silence*?

Q) Who was nicknamed 'The Bird'?

R) Give the date when **Glenn Miller** recorded *Moonlight Serenade*.

S) Where, and on what date, was **Duke Ellington** born?

T) Who are known as 'The Great Guitars'?

U) Name the **Oscar Peterson** (*Night Train*) **Trio.**

V) Who did **Diana Ross** portray in the movie *Lady Sings the Blues*?

W) Who scored in '76 with a cover of guitarist **Gabor Szabo's** *Breezin'*?

X) Name the instruments you associate with this list of musicians:

1. **Herbie Mann**
2. **Stephane Grappelly**
3. **Thelonious Monk**
4. **Sonny Rollins**
5. **Joe Pass**
6. **Max Roach**
7. **Cal Tjader**
8. **Stanley Clarke**
9. **Art Pepper**
10. **Gerry Mulligan**

Y) Who gave us *Fever* in '58?

Z) Name the influential record label founded by **Creed Taylor.**

Elton John

Right: Lesley Gore (*see* 74. K)

74 Rock All-Sorts
(General; worth 2 points each)

A) Name the group who parodied **The Shangri-Las'** *Leader of the Pack* hit under the title *Leader of the Laundromat.*
B) Which record company helped produce **Ken Kesey's** *One Flew Over the Cuckoo's Nest* movie ?
C) Who scored with the '72 *Mary C. Brown and The Hollywood Sign* album ?
D) What was the name of the white lady bass player who featured on the best of **Motown's** sixties' hits ?
E) Who formed **The Blackbyrds** ?
F) Name the group who scored in the early seventies with the *Have You Seen Her* hit single ?
G) Who sang the '62 *Baby It's Cold Outside* duet with **Ray Charles** ?
H) Which group originally recorded the classic *Save The Last Dance For Me* hit ?
I) Who penned and produced **Side Effect's** *Keep That Same Old Feeling* disco smash ?
J) In '75, who didn't **Johnny 'Guitar' Watson** want to be ?
K) What was the title of **Lesley Gore's** '63 number one hit single ?
L) Who in '58 had *Dinner with Drac* ?
M) Give the title of **Robin Ward's** one-off summer hit.
N) Who did **Bobby Vee** front on the '59 *Suzie Baby* single ?
O) Name **The Turtles'** biggest hit.
P) Who was the pianist

73 Starfile/Elton John
(Specialist; worth 3 points each)

A) Where, and on what date, was **Elton John** born ?
B) Give the name of his Harrow-based semi-pro group.
C) He met **Bernie Taupin** while working at which music publishing company ?
D) Give the title of his debut album.
E) Name the '72 **Ringo Starr** film in which he made a guest appearance.
F) What was his first US number one hit single ?
G) Name the record company he formed in '73.
H) **Marilyn Monroe** was the subject of which song ?
I) Who joined him on disc for his first UK number one hit single ?
J) Give the title of his big '78 (mainly) instrumental hit.

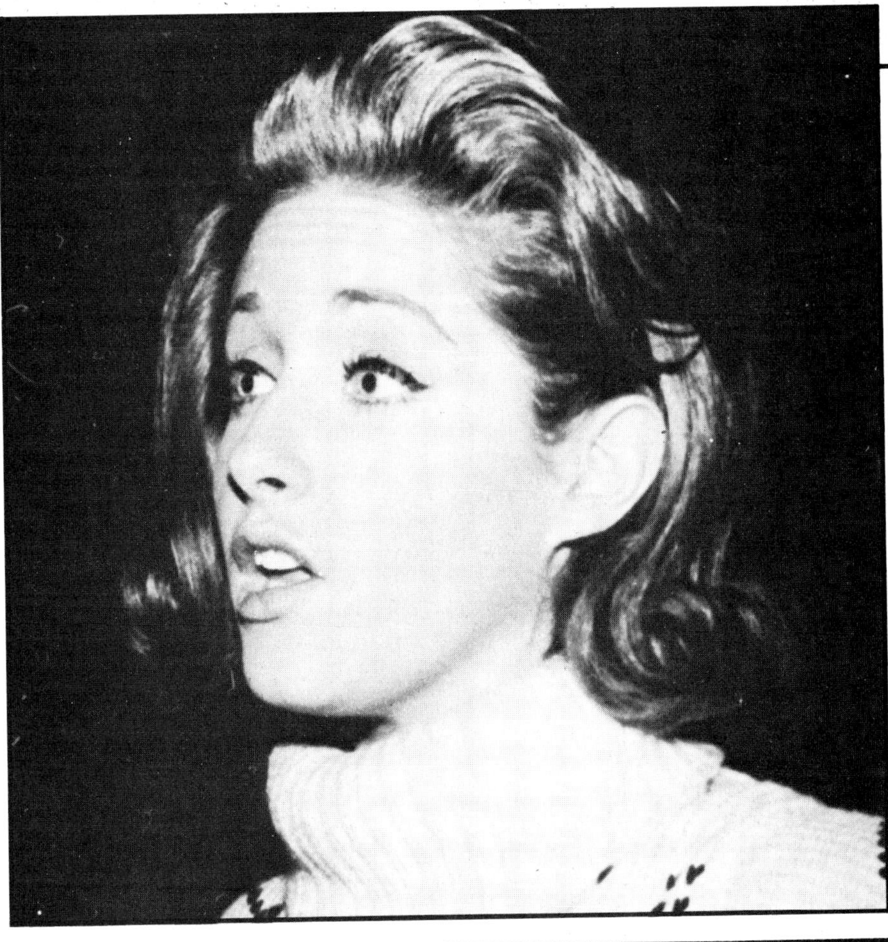

featured on **Presley's** *Heartbreak Hotel*?

Q) What are the surnames of **Peter, Paul and Mary,** and what was the title of their '78 reunion album?

R) **Chris Montez** scored his

two biggest hits in '62 and '66. What were their titles?

S) Name the individual **Rooftop Singers.**

T) Name the popular singer with a chain of hit records to his credit who once played drums for Country star **Faron Young.**

U) *Barefootin'* became a big hit for what ex-sax player?

V) Who scored in '75 with *Love is a Drug*?

W) Give the title of **The Mixtures'** 1970 hit single.

X) Who led the orchestra that scored in 1960 with the *Theme From A Summer Place*?

Y) How many times between '55 and '74 has **Bill Haley's** *Rock Around The Clock* crept into the UK top twenty?

Z) **Lorne Green,** star of TV's *Bonanza*, scored a hit single in '64. Give its title.

75 Disco Music

(Specialist; worth 3 points each)

A) Who penned **Chic's** big disco and chart successes?

B) Name the orchestra which recorded their best mid-seventies work under the musical guidance of arranger and conductor **Vincent Montano Jr.**

C) Give the title of **Norma Jean Wright's** debut single on the **Bearsville** label.

D) Who recorded a disco tribute to **Pink Floyd**?

E) What was **Rose Royce's** follow-up to their *Wishing On A Star* hit single?

F) Who produced **Starbooty's** '78 *Ubiquity* album?

G) Give the title of **Judge Dread's** '79 debut disco single.

H) Who penned the *Saturday Night Fever* movie soundtrack?

I) Name the jazz tenor-sax-man who crossed over for the '78 *Disco Dancing* single success.

J) Who co-penned the *You Make Me Feel (Mighty Real)* hit?

76 Starfile/ David Essex

(Specialist; worth 3 points each)

A) Name the group he formed in '64.

B) Give the title of his debut disc.

C) Name the group with whom he recorded *This Little Girl of Mine*.

D) Who did he understudy in the '69 London Palladium pantomime, *Dick Whittington*?

E) Name the movie in which he made his screen debut.

F) Which year was he the star of *Godspell*?

G) Which character did he portray in both *That'll Be the Day* and *Stardust*?

H) Who helped him cut the disc titled *Rock On*?

I) Name his first UK number one hit single.

J) Which award-winning stage musical brought him much personal acclaim in '78?

Below: The Sex Pistols (see 77. O)

77 The Crest of a Wave

(Specialist; worth 3 points each)

The US and UK New Wave scene became the most exciting, refreshing, energetic and original music force to hit rock since the golden sixties.

A) Which ex-**Velvet Underground** member has been dubbed 'The Godfather of Punk'?

B) What nationality was **Jonathan Richman's** Reggae?

C) Who scored in '77 with *Spanish Stroll*?

D) Which group includes **Pete Shelley** on lead vocals and guitar?

E) Whose music has been tagged 'The Sound of the Westway'?

F) Name **Wayne County's** group.

G) Under what name is **Johnny Jones** better known?

H) What was the title of the **Elvis Costello** album that featured his *Red Shoes* single?

I) Who sings with **The Blockheads**?

J) Where did **The Rezillos** hail from?

K) What type of musician is referred to in **Tonight's** hit single?

L) Before joining **The Ramones, March Bell** had previously been a member of which group?

M) What was the title of **The Angels'** hit which **Bette Bright and The Illuminations** re-vamped in '78?

N) Which **Patti Smith** track was included on *The Sire Machine Turns You Up* '78 album?

O) Name the '77 **Sex Pistols'** line-up.

P) Which member of **The Jam** burnt a copy of the *Sniffin' Glue* fanzine on stage at the Marquee club after the mag had described the group as "laid back"?

Q) Johnny, Joey, Dee Dee and Tommy were all what?

R) Name **Tom Petty's** group.

S) Under what name is **Chris Miller** better known?

T) Which group features **Billy Idol** as vocalist?

U) What ex-member of **Brinsley Schwarz** released the *I Made An American Squirm* single in '78?

V) Give the title of **Moon Martin's** '78 album.

W) Under what name did **The Stilettoes** become better known?

X) Who sings with **The Modern Lovers**?

Y) Who is **James Osterberg** better known as?

Z) Name four out of the eight groups that appeared on the '76 *Live At CBGB's* album.

78 Starfile/Elvis Costello

(Specialist; worth 3 points each)

A) Which '75 group featured **Elvis** as lead singer ?

B) Give one out of the two names which **Elvis** hadbeen known to use prior to his debut single.

C) In which year was the *Alison/Welcome To The Working Week* single released ?

D) Name the individual **Attractions.**

E) Give the title of his July '77 debut album.

F) Who produced the *This Year's Model* set ?

G) What two labels has **Elvis** recorded on ?

H) Which Fender guitar model is closely associated with him ?

I) What was the title of his late '78 hit single ?

J) Name the tracks that were featured on the *Live At Hollywood High* limited edition extended play.

Right: Carly Simon (*see* 79. A)

79 Rock All-Sorts

(General; worth 2 points each)

A) The stars listed below have all had hits with theme songs from **James Bond** movies. Name the songs they sang.
1. **Matt Monro**
2. **Shirley Bassey**
3. **Tom Jones**
4. **Nancy Sinatra**
5. **Paul McCartney and Wings**
6. **Carly Simon**

B) Who scored in '62 with *Nut Rocker*?

C) What was the title of **Francoise Hardy's** '65 English language hit?

D) How many UK number one hit singles did **Cliff Richard** notch up in the decade between '59 and '69?

E) What dish did **Tony Joe White** introduce us to in '69?

F) Who in '78 were *Dancing in the City*?

G) Which Rock 'n' Roll guitarist credited blues singer **Hambone** as a direct influence?

H) Who penned both **The Beatles'** *Anna* and **The Rolling Stones'** *You Better Move On?*

I) What group did **Stevie Winwood** form after his

departure from **The Spencer Davis Group**?

J) Who sang with **The Luvers**?

K) Give the title of **Trini Lopez's** big '63 hit single.

L) **A Taste of Honey** is fronted by two girls as bass player and lead guitarist. What are their names?

M) Who in '78 sang about *The Man With The Child In His Eyes*?

N) Name **Merle Haggard's** backing group.

O) Who penned **John Travolta and Olivia Newton John's** big *Summer Nights* hit from the *Grease* soundtrack?

P) What group of singers scored in '69 with *Oh Happy Day*?

Q) Name the individual members of **Blind Faith.**

R) Who in '64 liked *Bread and Butter*?

S) What are Chaw Mank, Little Buddies, King of Our Hearts and Blue Hawaiians?

T) *Nothing Rhymed* for who in 1970?

U) Who penned **The Spencer Davis Group's** *Keep On Running* and *Somebody Help Me* hits?

V) Who is **Susan Webb's** singer/songwriter brother?

W) Which group released the *Tales from Topographic Oceans* album?

X) Which record label uses a Red Indian on a horse as their logo?

Y) **The Allman Brothers Band** once had two real brothers in their line-up. What were their names?

Z) Who in '76 had an *Uptown Uptempo Woman*?

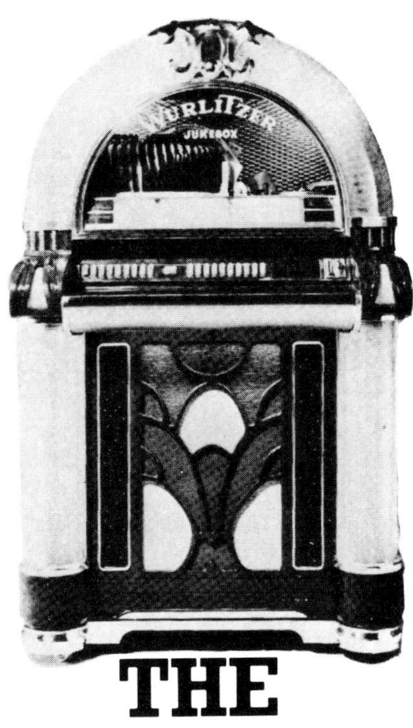

THE ANSWERS

1 Rock All-Sorts

(A) Annifred Lyngstad, Benny Anderson, Bjorn Ulvaeus, Agnetha Faltskog. (B) Duane Eddy. (C) Wall of Sound. (D) Barry, Robin, Maurice, Andy. (E) All scored with The 'In' Crowd. (F) Tom & Jerry. (G) Less Than Zero/Radio Sweetheart. (H) Cambridge, England. (I) The Cavern. (J) Mormon. (K) The Beatles. (L) Cass Elliot, Michelle Phillips, Denny Doherty, John Phillips. (M) Watford. (N) Hawthorne, Southern California. (O) Sheena. (P) Russia. (Q) Uncle Bob's Midnight Blues. (R) John Entwistle. (S) Ruth, Anita, Bonnie, June. (T) Pat Boone. (U) Where the Boys Are. (V) Carly Simon. (W) Yasgur's dairy farm, New York State. (X) Doo-Wop. (Y) Bill Haley. (Z) 1 June 1967.

2 Hail, Hail, Rock 'n' Roll

(A) Chuck Berry. (B) Blue Suede Shoes. (C) Alan Freed. (D) Charles Hardin Holley. (E) The Diamonds. (F) Blackboard Jungle. (G) Let's Get Together; C'mon Everybody. (H) The Rebels. (I) Phil Spector, Annette Bard, Marshall Lieb. (J) The Big Bopper. (K) William John Clifton Haley. (L) Maybellene. (M) Macon, Georgia; Richard Wayne Penniman. (N) Federal. (O) Flying Saucer. (P) Organ. (Q) Blue Caps. (R) American history and practical maths. (S) Jerry Lee Lewis. (T) At The Hop. (U) Don and Phil. (V) 1953. (W) Bobby Day. (X) Jamboree. (Y) Sal Mineo. (Z) Buddy Holly, Ritchie Valens and The Big Bopper; 3 February 1959.

3 Superstars/Elvis Presley

(A) Tupelo, Mississippi, January 8 1935. (B) Elvis Aaron Presley. (C) Thirteen. (D) Truck Driver. (E) Sam Phillips. (F) Sun. (G) Scotty Moore, Bill Black. (H) "Colonel" Thomas Andrew Parker. (I) Heartbreak Hotel, 1956. (J) All Shook Up, 1957. (K) Gracelands, Elvis Presley Boulevard. (L) 24/3/58-4/3/60. (M) Yes; a stop-over in Scotland while returning to the States from army service in Germany. (N) It's Now or Never. (O) Priscilla Beaulieu, April 30 1967. (P) Lisa Marie. (Q) August 16 1977.

4 Presley films

(A) David Weisbard; Love Me Tender. (B) Nine. (C) Don Siegel; Flaming Star. (D) 1. Flaming Star. 2. Kid Galahad. 3. Change of Habit. 4. Live a Little, Love a Little. 5. It Happened at the World's Fair. 6. The Trouble with Girls. 7. Easy Come Easy Go. 8. GI Blues.

5 Starfile/Bobby Darin

(A) Don Kirshner. (B) Splish Splash. (C) Mack The Knife; That's All. (D) Sandra Dee. (E) Come September; If A Man Answers; That Funny Feeling. (F) Come September. (G) Terry Melcher. (H) Pressure Point. (I) If I Were a Carpenter. (J) December '73.

6 Hail, Hail, Rock 'n' Roll

(A) Roy Orbison. (B) The Great Pretender. (C) Sherman Games, Joe Negroni, Herman Santiago, Jimmy Merchant. (D) Dorsey. (E) Elbows and Knees. (F) Moondog's Rock and Roll Party. (G) Elvis Presley, Jerry Lee Lewis, Carl Perkins, Johnny Cash. (H) Sweet Little Sixteen. (I) Gallatin, Tennessee. (J) Buddy Knox. (K) Green-eyed Mountain Jack. (L) July 1956, WF1L-TV, Philadelphia. (M) Bo Diddley. (N) Have Gun, Will Travel. (O) Fabiano Forte Bonaparte. (P) 17 April 1960. (Q) The Girl Can't Help It. (R) The Crickets. (S) Antoine 'Fats' Domino. (T) Bill Haley's Comets. (U) The Bo Diddley Beat. (V) Johnny and the Hurricanes. (W) Jimmy Bowen and Buddy Knox. (X) The Ballad of Stack-O-Lee. (Y) The Upsetters; I'm In Love Again, Every Night About This Time, Freedom Ride, Valley of Tears. (Z) Jack Scott.

7 Rock All-Sorts

(A) Nilsson Schmilsson, Son of Schmilsson, A Touch of Schmilsson in the Night. (B) John Denver. (C) Outside Buckingham Palace. (D) James Taylor. (E) Kookie Kookie (lend me your comb); Hawaiian Eye. (F) David Grusin. (G) Randy Scouse Git. (H) Five-A-Side. (I) Vincent Van Gogh. (J) Ambrose Slade. (K) Wink Martindale. (L) Living in the World of Broken Hearts. (M) Richard Berry and The Pharaohs. (N) Safe as Milk. (O) Elvis Costello. (P) Mala. (Q) Colin Blunstone. (R) Jimmy Cliff. (S) Sabre Dance; Dave Edmunds. (T) Paul Williams. (U) Harper's Bizarre. (V) Donna Summer. (W) Eva Narcissus Boyd. (X) Glen Campbell. (Y) Bobby Hebb's Sunny; The Beach Boys' Warmth of the Sun. (Z) Bryan 'Chas' Chandler.

8 Who are they ?

(A) Del Shannon. (B) Connie Francis. (C) Alice Cooper. (D) Cliff Richard. (E) Dusty Springfield. (F) Lou Christie. (G) Cat Stevens. (H) Ben E. King. (I) Sandie Shaw. (J) Bobby Darin. (K) Elton John. (L) Englebert Humperdink. (M) Pat Boone. (N) Bobbie Gentry. (O) David Bowie. (P) Tab Hunter. (Q) Johnny Rotten. (R) Dodie Stevens. (S) Conway Twitty. (T) Ritchie Valens. (U) Lulu. (V) Brook Benton. (W) Freddy Cannon. (X) Chris Farlowe. (Y) Bobby Rydell. (Z) Chubby Checker.

9 Starfile/Buddy Holly

(A) Lubbock, Texas, September 7 1936. (B) Bob Montgomery. (C) Decca. (D) Nashville, Tennessee. (E) Buddy, Sony Curtis, Jerry Allison. (F) Norman Petty. (G) The Crickets. (H) Maria Elena Santiago. (I) It Doesn't Matter Anymore. (J) Brown-Eyed Handsome Man.

10 They were really rockin' in Bolton

(A) Cliff Richard. (B) The Drifters; Hank B. Marvin, Bruce Welch, Jet Harris, Tony Meehan. (C) Billy Fury. (D) Frederick Heath; Johnny Kidd. (E) Shannon. (F) That'll Be The Day; Play It Cool. (G) Tommy Steele. (H) Saturday Night at the

Duck Pond. (I) Alvin Stardust. (J) The Human Jungle. (K) Joe Brown. (L) Besame Mucho; the Main Title Theme from The Man with the Golden Arm. (M) Holloway Road, London, England. (N) Heinz Burt; Just Like Eddie. (O) Jerry Lordan. (P) Beat Girl. (Q) Old Crompton St., Soho, London, England. (R) Geoff and Ricky; Warpaint. (S) Valerie Mountain and The Eagles. (T) A fox. (U) Larry Parnes. (V) Telstar. (W) Terry Dene. (X) Hit and Miss. (Y) 1. Wildcats. 2. Bruisers. 3. Pirates. 4. Outlaws. 5. Fentones. (Z) Jack Good.

11 Who's Who in Rock Movies

(A) Gary Glitter. (B) Pat Boone. (C) Leonard Cohen. (D) Elvis Presley. (E) Billy Fury. (F) Alan Price. (G) Harry Nilsson, Ringo Starr. (H) Chubby Checker. (I) The Dave Clark Five. (J) Bobby Darin. (K) Marc Bolan. (L) John Travolta, Olivia Newton-John. (M) Fabian. (N) Duane Eddy. (O) Diana Ross. (P) John & Yoko. (Q) Connie Francis. (R) Roy Orbison. (S) James Darren, The Four Preps. (T) Gerry and the Pacemakers. (U) Andy Williams. (V) Cliff Richard. (W) Bob Dylan. (X) Ray Charles. (Y) Arlo Guthrie. (Z) Bobby Rydell.

12 Oscar Winning Hits

(A) Raindrops Keep Fallin' On My Head, Music: Burt Bacharach, Lyrics: Hal David. (B) Theme from Shaft, Music & Lyrics by Isaac Hayes.

13 Hail, Hail, Rock 'n' Roll

(A) W. Davis, C. Patrick, G. Malone. (B) Drums. (C) The Southern Drifters. (D) Mark; Teen Angel. (E) Clovis, New Mexico. (F) Paul & Paula. (G) The Girl Can't Help It, Untamed Youth, Go Johnny Go, Bop Girl. (H) Ronald Bright. (I) Del-Fi Records. (J) Hippy Hippy Shake. (K) Johnny Tillotson. (L) 17yrs 9 mnths. (M) Norfolk, Virginia. (N) Short Fat Fannie, Bony Moronie, Dizzy Miss Lizzy. (O) 1959. (P) Accokeek. (Q) Crossfire. (R) 1. The Crests. 2. The Coasters. 3. Frankie Lyman and the Teenagers. 4. The Marcels. 5. The Skyliners. 6. Dell-Vikings. 7. Chantels. 8. The Crew Cuts. 9. The Spaniels. 10. The Five Satins. (S) Jackie De Shannon and Sharon Sheeley. (T) The Robins. (U) Brenda Lee. (V) Oooby Dooby. (W) The Alamo; North To Alaska. (X) Sam 'The Man' Taylor. (Y) Bullmoose. (Z) Lloyd Price.

14 Starfile/Pat Boone

(A) Daniel Boone. (B) Arthur Godfrey's Talent Scout Show. (C) Randy Wood. (D) Two Hearts, Two Kisses. (E) Shirley Jones. (F) I Almost Lost My Mind, Don't Forbid Me, April Love, Moody River. (G) Journey to the Center of the Earth. (H) Speedy Gonzales. (I) Terry Melcher. (J) Tamla Motown Organization.

15 Hail, Hail, Rock 'n' Roll

(A) The Adventures of Ozzie and Harriet. (B) Andy Williams. (C) Teddy Bear. (D) Philadelphia. (E) The Singin' Idol. (F) Like I Love You. (G) Dolton. (H) Jerry Lee Lewis. (I) The United Nations. (J) Felice and Boudleaux Bryant. (K) Twenty-six. (L) Eddie Cochran. (M) Ottawa, Canada. (N) 122 hrs 8 mins; Jape-A-Thon. (O) Disc Jockey Jamboree. (P) The Kalin Twins. (Q) Fever; Talk To Me, Talk To Me. (R) Henry Mancini. (S) Boom Boom. (T) Dion Di Mucci. (U) The Don'ts. (V) Seven. (W) K. C. Loving. (X) Jerry Keller. (Y) Rocko and his Saints. (Z) James Darren.

16 Rock All-Sorts

(A) Scott Engel, John Maus, Gary Leeds. (B) The Eagles. (C) The Twist. (D) Herb Alpert and Jerry Moss. (E) Alan, Wayne, Merrill, Jay, Donny, Jimmy. (F) The Last Time; Under My Thumb, 1967. (G) Sergeant Preston of the Yukon. (H) 1. Los Angeles. 2. London. 3. New York. 4. Liverpool. (I) Darogoi Dlimmoyo. (J) The Beach Boys. (K) Lee Hazlewood. (L) Wind in the Willows. (M) Marquee Club. (N) The Dakotas; The Cruel Sea. (O) Joe Dowell. (P) All scored with Stay. (Q) Rod Stewart. (R) The Hope & Anchor, London, England. (S) The Rutles. (T) Dark Horse. (U) Cardiff, Wales. (V) The French Connection. (W) Gene McDaniels. (X) Flowers in your hair. (Y) Prince Buster and the All Stars. (Z) The Move's Flowers in the Rain.

17 Superstars/The Beatles

(A) 1956. (B) John Lennon, Paul McCartney, George Harrison, Stuart Sutcliffe, Pete Best. (C) Drums. (D) Larry Parnes. (E) Bert Kaempfert. (F) December '61. (G) August '62. Rory Storme and the Hurricanes. (H) George Martin; Parlaphone. (I) Love Me Do. (J) Helen Shapiro. (K) Penny Lane/Strawberry Fields Forever. (L) His Own Write '64; A Spaniard in the Works '65. (M) Cry For A Shadow; Flying. (N) November '63. (O) Del Shannon; From Me To You. (P) 50,000; Ed Sullivan. (Q) On the set of A Hard Day's Night. (R) Richard Lester. (S) Keith Richard, Bill Wyman, Brian Jones. (T) MBEs. (U) I Want to Hold Your Hand; I Saw Her Standing There. (V) Shea Stadium. (W) Boys; Please Please Me. (X) The Roof, Apple Corps, Saville Row, London, England. (Y) I Knew Right Away. (Z) John Lennon.

18 Encore Quiz/The Beatles

(A) The fifth Beatle. (B) Bernard Webb and A. Smith. (C) Ravi Shankar. (D) Alleged overt drug allusions. (E) July '67; All You Need Is Love. (F) Bangor, Wales. (G) Maharishi Mahesh Yogi. (H) How I Won the War. (I) Baker Street, London, England. (J) Derek Taylor. (K) March '69. (L) George and Ringo. (M) Billy Preston. (N) Candy. (O) Boxing Day '67. (P) George Dunning. (Q) Only A Northern Song; All Together Now; Hey Bulldog; It's All Too Much. (R) Hey Jude/Revolution. (S) Yes It Is. (T) John Lennon. (U) San Francisco. (V) I Call Your Name; Slow Down; Matchbox. (W) Michael Lindsay-Hogg. (X) No One's Gonna Change Our World. (Y) Allen Klein. (Z) Abbey Road.

19 Mystery Openers

(A) Think. (B) Short People. (C) Tomorrow. (D) Scotland. (E) Twist and Shout. (F) Hello, I Love You. (G) The Bourgeois Blues. (H) Singing Winds, Crying Beasts. (I) Music For Money. (J) Like A Rolling Stone. (K) Miss You. (L) Goin' Back. (M) You Make Me Feel (Mighty Real). (N) That Loving Feeling. (O) Une Nuit à Paris (parts 1-3). (P) Get Ourselves Together. (Q) Shadoogie. (R) Ole Man Trouble. (S) Cotton fields. (T) The Fuse. (U) Silent Treatment. (V) Second hand News. (W) I Just Want To Have Something To Do. (X) Going Down On Love. (Y) No Action. (Z) Rock 'n' Roll Never Forgets.

20 Beatle Music Puzzle

(A) 2. Twist and Shout (Medley/Russell); 4. Devil In Her Heart (Drapkin); 9. Something (Harrison).

(B) Octopus's Garden. (C) His Elephant and Gun. (D) Kirkcaldy. (E) Taxman, Love You Too, I Want To Tell You. (F) The Daily Mail. (G) Four Thousand. (H) Van Morrison/ John Russell. (I) A banker with a motor car. (J) Wigwam. (K) What Goes On, from Rubber Soul. (L) Far away. (M) Here Comes The Sun. (N) Elementary Penguin. (O) John: I'm The Greatest; Paul: Six o'clock; George: Sunshine Life for Me. (P) Phil Spector and George Martin. (Q) I Want You (She's so heavy). (R) 1. Michelle. 2. Girl. 3. You've Got To Hide Your Love Away. 4. If I Needed Someone. 5. With A Little Help from My Friends. 6. Got To Get You Into My Life. 7. Norwegian Wood. 8. When I'm Sixty-four. 9. Do You Want to Know A Secret? 10. Ob-La-Di-Ob-La-Da.

21 Starfile/The Moody Blues

(A) Denny Laine, Mike Pinder, Graham Edge, Ray Thomas, Clint Warwick. (B) Lose Your Money. (C) Alex Murray. (D) The Magnificent Moodies '65. (E) Justin Hayward and John Lodge. (F) Threshold. (G) Autum '68. (H) Days of Future Passed. (I) Lodge and Hayward. (J) Ray Thomas.

22 Rock All-Sorts

(A) Paul Williams. (B) Concrete and Clay. (C) Andy Fairweather Lowe. (D) Swedish. (E) 16. (F) It's All In The Game. (G) Ruth Brown. (H) Johnny Mathis. (I) Does Your Chewing Gum Loose its Flavour (on the bed-post over night) ? (J) The Palladium Theatre. (K) 1964. (L) Colin Peterson. (M) Young Love. (N) Gary Puckett. (O) Them. (P) Mike Chapman, Nicky Chinn. (Q) The Mindbenders. (R) Brian Poole. (S) Tottenham, London, England. (T) Theme From Dr. Kildare (Three Stars Will Shine Tonight). (U) Merthyr Tydfil, South Wales; 98.6. (V) Leif Garrett. (W) No Regrets. (X) The Yardbirds. (Y) Bette Bright and the Illuminations. (Z) Leitch.

23 Starfile/The Who

(A) Roger Daltrey, Pete Townshend, John Enthwistle, Keith Moon. (B) The Oldfield Hotel, Greenford, Middlesex, England. (C) The Mods. (D) Shel Talmy. (E) I Can't Explain. (F) The Ox. (G) John Entwistle. (H) Ken Russell. (I) Leeds. (J) Kenny Jones.

24 The Beat Scene

(A) How Do You Do It?; I Like It; You'll Never Walk Alone. (B) Herman's Hermits. (C) Newcastle. (D) Tom Jones. (E) Peter Gunn. (F) Ronnie 'Plonk' Lane, Steve Marriot, Kenny Jones, Ian McLaglan. (G) Mike D'Abo. (H) 1964. (I) Hedgehoppers Anonymous. (J) Colour of My Love. (K) The Cruisers. (L) Scream and Scream Again. (M) Over and Over. (N) George Martin. (O) I Put A Spell On You. (P) Ray Davies, Dave Davies, Mick Avory, Peter Quaife. (Q) John Ford's Western movie. (R) Ain't That Just Like Me. (S) Freddie and The Dreamers. (T) Erith, Kent, England. (U) The Cavern Club. (V) Lennon; McCartney. (W) 1964. (X) Italy. (Y) Sounds Incorporated. (Z) The Big Three.

25 Who are they?

(A) Guy Mitchell. (B) Ricky Nelson. (C) Jet Harris. (D) Bobby Vee. (E) Dinah Washington. (F) The Allisons. (G) Ringo Starr. (H) Johnny Hallyday. (I) James Darren. (J) Little Eva. (K) Gary US Bonds. (L) Billy J. Kramer. (M) Stevie Wonder. (N) Gene Chandler. (O) Cilla Black. (P) Georgie Fame. (Q) Chris Montez. (R) Denny Laine. (S) Len Barry. (T) Wayne Fontana. (U) Sam the Sham. (V) Jackie De Shannon. (W) Tom Jones. (X) Vicki Carr. (Y) Adam Faith. (Z) Billy Fury.

26 Superstars/The Rolling Stones

(A) December '62. (B) Andrew Oldham. (C) Mick Jagger, Charlie Watts, Keith Richard, Brian Jones, Bill Wyman. (D) Come On/I Wanna Be Loved. (E) June 7 1963; Thank Your Lucky Stars. (F) The Everly Brothers, Bo Diddley and Little Richard. (G) I Wanna Be Your Man. (H) Gene Pitney. (I) Not Fade Away; Buddy Holly. (J) Charlie 'Bird' Parker. (K) (I Can't Get No) Satisfaction. (L) The TAMI Show. (M) Allen Klein. (N) As Tears Go By. (O) Palace of Culture, Warsaw, Poland. (P) We Love You. (Q) Rock 'n' Roll Circus. (R) June 8 1969. (S) Honky Tonk Woman. (T) July 3 1969. (U) Performance. (V) Glenrowen, Melbourne, Australia. (W) Bianca Perez Morena de Macias. (X) Brown Sugar/Bitch/Let It Rock, maxi single. (Y) Andy Warhol; Sticky Fingers. (Z) Ronnie Wood.

27 Rock All-Sorts

(A) My Little Town. (B) Room 1472, Hotel La Reine Elizabeth, Montreal, Canada. (C) John Sebastian, Steve Boone, Joe Butler, Zalman Yanovsky. (D) Rick Derringer. (E) Don't Bring Lulu; The Roaring Twenties. (F) Jerry Leiber, Mike Stoller. (G) (Ghost) Riders In The Sky. (H) 1. Wendy Richard. 2. Billie Davis. (I) Sheila ('62); Dizzy ('69). (J) Stone Alone. (K) Saturday Night Fever. (L) Althia and Donna. (M) Skateboard. (N) Boney M. (O) Mick Jagger and Keith Richard. (P) I Love My Dog. (Q) Not To Be Taken Away. (R) Brenten Wood. (S) Sandie Shaw. (T) Brian Hyland. (U) Ride The Wild Surf. (V) The Poni-Tails. (W) Merry-Go-Round. (X) In The Year 2525. (Y) 4 - I Remember You; Lovesick Blues; Wayward Wind; Confessin'. (Z) David 'Hutch' Soul.

28 Starfile/Jimi Hendrix

(A) The Isley Brothers. (B) New York '65. (C) Noel Redding (bass) and Mitch Mitchell (drums). (D) Hey Joe. (E) Sweden. (F) November '68. (G) Woodstock. (H) The Fillmore East. (I) Bass player Billy Cox became ill and was unable to perform. (J) September 18 1970.

29 Black Music

(A) Carla Thomas. (B) 125th Street, Harlem, New York City. (C) Sam Cooke. (D) Memphis Group. (E) Bobby McClure. (F) Smokey Robinson. (G) A Lover's Concerto, based on a Bach melody. (H) Tommy Tucker; Hi Heel Sneakers. (I) McLemore Avenue, Memphis, Tennessee. (J) Lee Dorsey. (K) Ray Charles Robinson. (L) Berry Gordy. (M) The Miracles Shop Around. (N) 1. Mary Wells. 2. Kim Weston. 3. Tammi Terrell. 4. Diana Ross. (O) Erma Franklin; Piece of My Heart. (P) Barry White; Relf and Nelson. (Q) Jackie, Tito, Jarmaine, Marlon, Michael, Randy. (R) Alabama; Steve Cropper. (S) Braddock. (T) Hank Ballard. (U) St. Louis Blues. (V) Otis and the Shooters; She's Alright, 1959. (W) Sam Moore, Dave Prater. (X) Jim STewart and Estelle AXton. (Y) Willie Mitchell. (Z) Marcia Barratt, Liz Mitchell, Maizie Williams, Bobby Farrall.

30 Starfile/Otis Redding

(A) Dawson, Georgia. (B) Johnny Jenkins and The Pinetoppers. (C) Jim Stewart. (D) Volt. (E) The Rolling Stones. (F) Jerry Butler.

(G) Monterey Pop. (H) Day Tripper. (I) 26. (J) Dexter Redding; God Bless.

31 Black Music

(A) Rose Royce. (B) Nat King Cole. (C) Yesterday; Eleanor Rigby. (D) Butch, Ralph, Chubby, Tiny, Pooch. (E) Dock of The Bay. (F) Little. (G) G.C. Cameron. (H) Mother, Father, Sister, Brother. (I) Special Occasion. (J) Jarmaine. (K) The Apollo Theatre. (L) Curtis Mayfield. (M) Twistin' Postman. (N) Desmond Dekker. (O) Hey There Lonely Boy, performed by Ruby and The Romantics. (P) Earth, Wind and Fire. (Q) 1. Martha and The Vandellas. 2. The Isley Bros. 3. Stevie Wonder. 4. Marvin Gaye. 5. The Temptations. 6. Junior Walker and The All-Stars. 7. Mary Wells. 8. The Supremes. 9. The Four Tops. 10. Smokey Robinson and the Miracles. (R) Wet Dream. (S) Pluto Sherrington. (T) The 14th Annual Independence Celebration of Ghana. (U) Allen Toussaint and Marshall Sehorn. (V) Taj Mahal. (W) Rock Your Baby. (X) Boney M. (Y) Dance, Dance, Dance. (Z) Dave Crawford.

32 Starfile/The Supremes

(A) Your Heart Belongs To Me. (B) Baby Love. (C) The TAMI Show. (D) Cindy Birdsong. (E) A Bit of Liverpool. (F) Sam Cooke. (G) The Happening. (H) Reflections. (I) Mary Wilson; Up the Ladder to the Roof. (J) The Wiz.

33 Black Music

(A) The Detroit Spinners. (B) Charles Cooke; You Send Me. (C) King Curtis. (D) The Rockford Files. (E) Johnny Ace. (F) Levi Stubbs, Abdul 'Duke' Fakir, Renaldo Benson, Lawrence Payson. (G) Please, Please, Please. (H) Jimmy Forrest. (I) Thank You Falettinme, BeMice Elf Agin/Everybody Is a Star. (J) Diana Ross. (K) Beach Ball. (L) You'll Need Another Favor. (M) Ben Cauley. (N) The Intruders. (O) Thom Bell and Linda Creed. (P) Rudolph and Ronald O'Kelly. (Q) Bob Marley. (R) The Drifters. (S) Columbia. (T) Arthur Conley. (U) Close Encounters Of The Third Kind. (V) Take A Giant Step. (W) Ray Charles. (X) The Showstoppers; Ain't Nothin' But a House Party. (Y) The Dog/Walking The Dog. (Z) Chaka Khan.

34 Starfile/Booker T & The M.G.s

(A) 1962. (B) Lewis Steinberg. (C) Steve Cropper and Donald 'Duck' Dunn. (D) Green Onions. (E) My Sweet Potato; And Now. (F) Jingle Bells/Winter Wonderland; Silver Bells/Winter Snow. (G) Up Tight. (H) Bobby Manuel and Carson Whitsett. (I) Universal Language; Al Jackson. (J) Priscilla Collidge.

35 Rock All-Sorts

(A) The album includes a cover by Smith of The Weight instead of the original Band (film) version. (B) Something Else. (C) John D. Loudermilk. (D) Maggie May. (E) Seattle, Washington; James Marshall Hendrix. (F) Keith McCormack; Wheels. (G) Jeff Beck. (H) London. (I) Jazz. (J) I'm A Believer; A Little Bit Me, A Little Bit You. (K) The Parent Trap. (L) Waterloo. (M) The Golliwogs. (N) Dr. West's Medicine Show and Junk Band; The Eggplant That Ate Chicago (Go, Go). (O) Judge Dread. (P) The Byrds; Buffalo Springfield; The Hollies. (Q) The Rifleman. (R) Lobo. (S) Silver Star, Who Loves You, December 1963, (Oh What A Night). (T) My Best Friend's Girl; The Cars. (U) Fairweather. (V) Pratt and McClain. (W) Man of Words, Man of Music. (X) October 29 1964. (Y) Cafe Creme. (Z) It's Trad Dad.

36 Rock Movie Stars

(A) Peter Frampton, The Bee Gees. (B) Joan Baez. (C) Tommy Sands, Annette Funicello. (D) Cliff Richard. (E) Paul Anka. (F) Frankie Avalon. (G) Tommy Steele. (H) The Monkees. (I) The Rolling Stones. (J) Diana Ross. (K) Jerry Lee Lewis. (L) The Bonzo Dog Doo-Dah Band. (M) Herman's Hermits. (N) Waylon Jennings. (O) Adam Faith. (P) David Essex, Ringo Starr. (Q) Paul Jones. (R) Eddie Cochran. (S) Billy Fury. (T) Jimi Hendrix. (U) Joe Cocker, Leon Russell. (V) Ricky Nelson. (W) Curtis Mayfield. (X) Kris Kristofferson, Bob Dylan. (Y) Elvis Presley. (Z) Jimmy Cliff.

37 Oscar Winners

(A) Born Free. Music: John Barry, Lyrics: Don Black. (B) The Way We Were. Music: Marvin Hamlisch, Lyrics: Alan and Marilyn Bergman.

38 Superstars/The Beach Boys

(A) Brian, Carl and Dennis Wilson, Mike Love and Al Jardine. (B) Al Jardine. (C) Cousin. (D) Muscle Beach Party; Girls On the Beach; Ride the Wild Surf. (E) Girls on the Beach; William N. Whitney. (F) Surfer Girl. (G) Bruce & Terry; Terry Melcher. (H) Marilyn and Diane Rovell; The Honeys, American Spring. (I) Good Vibrations. (J) Smile. (K) Al Jardine. (L) Transcendental Meditation. (M) The Radiant Radish. (N) Stack O Tracks. (O) Dennis Wilson; Two Lane Blacktop. (P) Little Saint Nick; The Man with All the Toys; Child of Winter. (Q) Steve and Stan Love. (R) Mount Vernon and Fairway. (S) Brian Wilson, June 20 1942. Dennis Wilson, December 4 1944; Carl Wilson, December 21 1946; Mike Love, March 15 1941; Al Jardine, September 3 1942.

39 Who are they?

(A) Junior Walker. (B) P.J. Proby. (C) Smokey Robinson. (D) Crispian St. Peters. (E) Nina Simone. (F) Cher. (G) Edwin Starr. (H) Tammi Terrell. (I) Tiny Tim. (J) Doris Troy. (K) B.B. King. (L) Roy C. (M) Captain Beefheart. (N) Billie Davis. (O) Dave Dee. (P) Darlene Love. (Q) Barbara Lynn. (R) Mickie Most. (S) Sandy Posey. (T) Gilbert O'Sullivan. (U) Carole King. (V) Ian Matthews. (W) Gene Vincent. (X) Dr. John. (Y) Marc Bolan. (Z) Gary Glitter.

40 Rock All-Sorts

(A) The Dovells. (B) Shel Talmy. (C) Tyrannasaurus Rex. (D) 1964; Good Morning Little Schoolgirl; Decca. (E) Chuck Berry and Dave Berry; Memphis Tennessee. (F) Fleetwood Mac. (G) 7.22. (H) Diary of a Mad Housewife. (I) Ray Peterson's Corrina, Corrina. (J) Joe Cocker. (K) Rio, Brazil. (L) John Fogerty. (M) "Captain Daryl Dragon"; Toni Tennille. (N) Jackie De Shannon. (O) Blue Cats. (P) Johnny Ray. (Q) New Wave. (R) Bruce Johnston (S) Tomorrow. (T) David Cassidy. (U) Oh Neil. (V) The Who; I'm the Face/Zoot Suit. (W) Powerhouse. (X) Midnight Cowboy; Fred Neil. (Y) Frank Sinatra. (Z) Scotland.

41 Summer Means Fun (Surf/hot-rod music)

(A) The Turtles. (B) A curl of a wave before it breaks. (C) Willie and The Wheels. (D) Tony Hilder. (E) The Chantays. (F) Three Surfer Boys. (G) The Jesters. (H) To fall off your board. (I) Murry Wilson. (J) Boulder Colorado; Baja; Surf Party. (K) The Trashmen. (L) Mike Curb. (M) Hot Rod Rog. (N) My Buddy Seat. (O) Peter Anders and Vinnie Poncia. (P) Catch A Wave. (Q) All had bald heads. (R) Gary Usher. (S) Dick Dale and The Deltones. (T) Nashville, Tennessee. (U) Bruce Johnston and Terry Melcher. (V) New Girl In School. (W) Del-Fi. (X) The Sandals. (Y) The Fantastic Baggys. (Z) The Surfmen.

42 Starfile/Jan and Dean

(A) Jan Berry and Dean Torrence. (B) Arwin. (C) Lou Adler and Herb Alpert. (D) Jan's garage. (E) Tommy 'Snuff' Garrett. (F) Surfin'; Surfin' Safari. (G) Surf City. (H) The Anaheim and Azusa and Cucamonga Sewing Circle Book Review and Timing Association. (I) Bucket T. (J) Beverly Hills, Los Angeles, 1965.

43 Beach Boys' Music

(A) The Bad Guys. (B) Caroline No. (C) Spirit of America. (D) 1. Christian. 2. Usher. 3. Love. 4. Asher. 5. Parkes. 6. McGuinn. (E) John Steinbeck's Travels with Charley; Al Jardine.

44 Mystery Openers

(A) You Ain't Going Nowhere. (B) Welcome To My Nightmare. (C) Take It All. (D) I Got A Line On You. (E) If We Should Lose Our Love. (F) Last Date. (G) As Tears Go By. (H) Morning Morgantown. (I) Love's In Need of Love Today. (J) How Can This Be Love. (K) Big Barn Bed. (L) He's The One I Love. (M) Turn to Stone. (N) After the Storm. (O) Thank You for Sending Me an Angel. (P) Tambu (Tombo in 7/4). (Q) Wish I Was in Nashville. (R) Dance, Dance, Dance. (Yowsah, Yowsah, Yowsah.) (S) Any Way You Like It. (T) Miniature. (U) California Dreamin'. (V) Dune Buggy. (W) Johnny Strikes Up The Band. (X) Crop-Dustin. (Y) See See Rider. (Z) Love Comes to Everyone.

45 Starfile/The Surfaris

(A) Glendora, Southern California. (B) Jim Fuller, Ron Wilson, Pat Connolly, Bob Berryhill, Jim Pash. (C) Ron Wilson. (D) Dale Smallin. (E) Baja; Blue Surf. (F) The Lively Set. (G) Gary Usher. (H) It Ain't Me Babe. (I) Ken Forssi. (J) Show Biz Chicago Green.

46 Rock All-Sorts

(A) Jimmy Nicol. (B) The Yardbirds. (C) Vincebus Eruptum. (D) Jimmy. (E) Bobby Hatfield and Bill Medley. (F) Both were murdered by intruders in their homes. (G) Dee Dee Warwick. (H) To develop the Gizmo instrument. (I) Dusty in Memphis. (J) Phil Spector. (K) William Friedkin. (L) You're Moving Out Today. (M) David Gates. (N) John Conteh. (O) Bob Hite. (P) One; Sheb Wooley. (Q) Bruce Springsteen. (R) Little Feat. (S) Liverpool. (T) Nick Lowe. (U) Jackie; Jacques Brel. (V) Johnny Otis. (W) Greenwich Village. (X) Freda Payne. (Y) The Man who Fell to Earth. (Z) Judy Collins.

47 Starfile/The Byrds

(A) The Beefeaters. (B) Jim McGuinn, Chris Hillman, Gene Clark, David Crosby, Michael Clarke. (C) Terry Melcher; Mr. Tambourine Man. (D) Gene Clark. (E) Ciro's; The Trip. (F) 12-string Rickenbacker. (G) Gary Usher; The Notorious Byrd Brothers. (H) Catalog of Western Clothes. (I) International Submarine Band. (J) 1973.

48 L.A. Rock

(A) Honolulu International Center Arena, July '64. (B) Grass Roots; Arthur Lee; Ken Forssi. (C) Ballrooms. (D) Neil Young, Steve Stills, Richie Furay, Dewey Martin, Bruce Palmer. (E) Crosby, McGuinn, Hillman. (F) I Got You Babe. (G) Miami. (H) The Tikis. (I) Child of Our Times. (J) Van Nuys. (K) Stephen Stills. (L) 1. Jefferson Airplane; 2. Moby Grape; (M) June 1970; Ladies of the Canyon. (N) Ed Cassidy. (O) Van Dyke Parks. (P) The Trip. (Q) Other Voices. (R) TV Rock shows. (S) Lou Adler. (T) Creeque Alley. (U) 18.57. (V) I Love You Alice B. Toklas. (W) Harvey Brooks, Eddie Hoh, Barry Goldberg. (X) Gary Usher. (Y) United States of America. (Z) Freak Out.

49 Starfile/The Doors

(A) Jim Morrison, Ray Manzarek, Robby Kreiger, John Densmore. (B) Kreiger, Densmore. (C) The 1930 German Opera, The Rise and Fall of the City of Mahogany. (D) Light My Fire. (E) Doug Lubahn. (F) Hello I Love You. (G) New Haven, Connecticut. (H) L.A. Woman. (I) Paris, France July 3 1971. (J) An American Prayer.

50 Rock Duos

(A) Herb. (B) Bonnie. (C) Dean. (D) Paula. (E) Cher. (F) Tony. (G) Lee. (H) Dave. (I) Price. (J) Marcia. (K) Tennille. (L) Ansil Collins. (M) Grace. (N) Deedee. (O) Johnny. (P) Marie. (Q) Scruggs. (R) Charlie Foxx. (S) Jonathan. (T) Lyle. (U) Jeremy. (V) Lee. (W) Simpson. (X) Katie Kissoon. (Y) Tina Turner. (Z) Garfunkel.

51 Starfile/Mamas and Papas

(A) The Virgin Islands. (B) Barry McGuire. (C) California Dreamin'; If You Can Believe Your Eyes and Ears. (D) Monterey International Pop Festival. (E) John Phillips. (F) Cass Elliot. (G) People Like Us. (H) Brewster McCloud. (I) Valentino (J) London, July 29 1974.

52 Rock All-Sorts

(A) Your Generation. (B) Jack Nitszche. (C) Talking Heads. (D) The Winstons. (E) Leif Garrett. (F) Ring Ring. (G) The Damned. (H) Heddon Street, London W.1. (I) Jimmy Buffett. (J) Electric Light Orchestra. (K) Millington. (L) Jack Jones. (M) Photographer. (N) Sonny Rollins. (O) The London Palladium. (P) L.A. New Wave. (Q) Ian Dury. (R) The Equals. (S) Burt Bacharach and Hal David. (T) Elias and his Zigzag Jive Flutes. (U) The Thomas Crown Affair. (V) 1. drums. 2. bass guitar. (W) Georgie Fame. (X) Boston. (Y) Bruce Springsteen. (Z) Bette Midler.

53 Starfile/Nilsson

(A) Harry Edward Nilsson III. (B) Johnny Niles. (C) The Monkees. (D) Pandemonium Shadow Show. (E) The Ghost of Mrs Muir. (F) I Guess the Lord Must Be In New York City. (G) Little Cowboy/When We Go Marching Down Broadway. (H) A prison guard. (I) 1. George Tipton. 2. Richard Perry. 3. Derek Taylor. 4. John Lennon. (J) The Point.

54 Rock All-Sorts

(A) Mickey Dolenz. (B) San Francisco. (C) Howlin' Wolf. (D) Lovers of The World Unite. (E) Joan Baez. (F) Give Peace A Chance. (G) Chills and Fever. (H) Bobby Freeman. (I) Joseph Byrd. (J) New York and San Francisco; Bill Graham. (K)

Tony Orlando. (L) James Coburn, Michael Parkinson, Kenny Lynch, Clement Freud, Christopher Lee, John Conteh. (M) The Carpenters. (N) Tuff. (O) Herb Abramson and Ahmet Ertegun. (P) Waterloo. (Q) The Doobie Brothers. (R) Rapp. (S) Armed Forces. (T) The Fireballs. (U) Fred Milano, Carlo Mastangelo, Angelo D'Aleo. (V) Faithful. (W) Everybody Is A Star. (X) Michael McDonald. (Y) Edinburgh, Scotland; The Saxons. (Z) O.C. Smith.

55 Starfile/The Eagles

(A) Don Henley, Glenn Frey, Bernie Leadon, Randy Meisner. (B) Glenn Frey and Jackson Browne. (C) Olympic Studios, London, England. (D) Glyn Johns. (E) One of These Nights. (F) Don Felder. (G) 1976; Joe Walsh. (H) Randy Meisner. (I) Please Come Home for Christmas/Funky New Year. (J) Joe Walsh.

56 Superstars/Bob Dylan

(A) Robert Allen Zimmerman. (B) Dylan Thomas. (C) March '62. (D) Newport Folk Festival. (E) John Hammond. (F) Madhouse On Castle Street. (G) Joan Baez. (H) 1. Scarborough Fair; 2. Lord Randall; 3. Nottamun Town. (I) Tom Wilson. (J) Black Crow Blues; Another Side of Bob Dylan. (K) Lyndon B. Johnson. (L) It's Alright Ma (I'm Only Bleeding). (M) Newport. (N) D.A. Pennebaker. (O) The Byrds. (P) Triumph. (Q) Nashville; Blonde On Blonde; Sad Eyed Lady of The Lowlands. (R) Woody Guthrie. (S) John Wesley Harding. (T) £35,000. (U) Producer Bob Johnson. (V) The Band. (W) The Concert For Bangla Desh. (X) Tarantula. (Y) Pat Garrett & Billy The Kid. (Z) Changing of the Guards.

57 Rock All-Sorts

(A) Eden Kane/Well I Ask You; Peter Sarstedt/Where Do You Go To, My Lovely? ((B) John Lennon. (C) The Skatalites. (D) Steve Ellis. (E) Jay and The Techniques. (F) Davy Graham. (G) In the City. (H) Left Banke. (I) Paul Williams. (J) Slade. (K) The Box Tops. (L) Lynsey de Paul. (M) Virgin Records. (N) The Motors. (O) Elvis Costello and the Attractions. (P) From The Inside. (Q) His Rockabilly Rebels. (R) Jim Jacobs and Warren Casey. (S) Honey. (T) Trumpet. (U) Freddy Cannon. (V) Je t'Aime . . . Moi Non Plus. (W) Billy Preston. (X) The Cyrkle. (Y) 1962. (Z) Tony Macauley and Mike D'Abo.

58 Dylan Music

(A) The Basement. (B) The Boxer. (C) A little girl. (D) 1. Peter, Paul and Mary; 2. Manfred Mann; 3. Julie Driscoll and The Brian Auger Trinity; 4. The Byrds; 5. Jimi Hendrix Experience. (E) Man and God and Law. (F) Knockin' On Heaven's Door. (G) Talking John Birch Society Blues; Ramblin' Gamblin' Willy; Rock and Gravel; Let Me Die In My Footsteps. (H) Ringo Starr, George Harrison and Leon Russell. (I) I Shall Be Released. (J) I'd Have You Anytime.

59 Starfile/Simon and Garfunkel

(A) Tom & Jerry. (B) Motorcycle/Lisa. (C) Garfunkel (on the Octavia and Warwick labels). (D) Jerry Landis. (E) Dick Clark's American Bandstand. (F) Bridge Over Troubled Water. (G) Wednesday Morning 3 am. (H) Mike Nichols; Catch-22; Lieutenant Nately. (I) Bye Bye Love; Bridge Over Troubled Water. (J) Annie Hall.

60 Starfile/The Band

(A) Canada. (B) The Hawks; Ronnie Hawkins. (C) Robbie Robertson, Richard Manuel, Levon Helm, Garth Hudson, Rick Danko. (D) 1966. (E) Music from Big Pink; Bob Dylan. (F) 4% Pantomime, Cahoots. (G) Rag Mama Rag. (H) Moondog Matinee. (I) The Last Waltz. (J) Robbie Robertson.

61 Folk Music

(A) Fifty-ninth Street Bridge Song (Feelin' Groovy). (B) Bob Dylan. (C) Woodrow Wilson Guthrie. (D) Barry McGuire. (E) Greenwich Village, New York. (F) Idris Davies. (G) Catch The Wind. (H) Peter, Paul and Mary. (I) Been Down So Long It Looks Like Up to Me; Joan Baez. (J) Arlo Guthrie; Alice's Restaurant.

62 Starfile/Joan Baez

(A) Bill Wood and Ted Alevizos. (B) 1960. (C) 1962. (D) Institute for the Study of Non-Violence. (E) Richard Farina. (F) Draft evasion. (G) Joan. (H) Mimi Farina. (I) Daybreak. (J) Bob Dylan.

63 Starfile/James Taylor

(A) The Flying Machine. (B) Notting Hill Gate, London, England. (C) Paul McCartney. (D) Sweet Baby James. (E) Carole King. (F) Two Lane Blacktop. (G) Carly Simon. (H) Alex, Livingston, and Kate. (I) Lenny Waronker and Russ Titelman. (J) Boys in the Trees.

64 The Love Crowd

(A) Grace Slick. (B) Rick Griffin. (C) The Family Dog. (D) Quicksilver Messenger Service. (E) The Grateful Dead. (F) Light Shows. (G) Country Joe McDonald. (H) Big Brother and The Holding Company. (I) Steve Miller. (J) Somebody To Love; White Rabbit. (K) Texas. (L) Tom Donahue. (M) Jefferson Starship. (N) Summertime Blues. (O) To have a baby. (P) The Grateful Dead. (Q) The Airplane. (R) Moby Grape. (S) It's a Beautiful Day. (T) Creedence Clearwater Revival. (U) Poster artists. (V) Dan Hicks. (W) A dance organization. (X) October 3 1970. (Y) Steve Miller and Boz Scaggs. (Z) The Grateful Dead.

65 Rock All-Sorts

(A) Beckenham, Kent, England. (B) David Essex. (C) The Sheriff of Fractured Jaw. (D) The Kick Inside. (E) Millie Small. (F) Morgen. (G) Massachusetts. (H) The Birds. (I) Leap Up and Down (Wave Your Knickers in the Air). (J) The Stone Poneys. (K) 1966. (L) The Little Shepherd of Kingdom Come. (M) (The Man Who Shot) Liberty Valance; Town Wothout Pity. (N) Jan and Dean's From All Over the World. (O) Seals and Crofts. (P) Wax 'Em Down. (Q) Circus Boy. (R) Canada. (S) Bay City Rollers. (T) Let's Go. (U) Phil Sloan. (V) The Mugwumps. (W) Danny Hutton, Chuck Megron, Cory Wells. (X) The Four Seasons. (Y) The Apartment. (Z) Sandy Posey.

66 Country Music

(A) Crazy Tennesseans. (B) If I Were a Carpenter. (C) Hargus Robbins. (D) Bakerfield. (E) Waylon Jennings and The Waylors. (F) Foggy Mountain Breakdown. (G) Duane Eddy. (H) Steel Guitar. (I) Bill and Earl Bolick. (J) Kimberley Jim. (K) Sheb Wooley. (L) Jolene. (M) Willie Nelson, Jessi Colter, Tompall Glaser. (N) The Dopyera Brothers. (O) Harmonica. (P) C. W. McCall. (Q) Stand By Your Man. (R) George Hamilton. (S) True Grit. (T) Chet Atkins. (U) Skeeter Davis. (V) Piano. (W) The Most Beautiful Girl. (X) Uncle Dave Macon. (Y) The Pozo Seco Singers. (Z) Hank Snow.

67 Starfile/Johnny Cash

(A) Hey Porter/Cry Cry Cry. (B) Luther Perkins and Marshall Grant. (C) Five Minutes To Live. (D) W. S. Holland. (E) June Carter. (F) San Quentin. (G) Carl Perkins. (H) Bob Dylan's Nashville Skyline. (I) Johnny Cash, The Man and His Music. (J) Kirk Douglas.

68 Country Music

(A) Henson Cargill. (B) Saxophone. (C) Eddie Rabbitt. (D) Guitar Man; U.S. Male. (E) Bluegrass. (F) Crystal Gayle. (G) 1961. (H) Hank Williams. (I) 4 Music Square East, Nashville, Tennessee. (J) June Carter and Merle Kilgore. (K) King of the Road. (L) Waylon Jennings. (M) Cajun. (N) Tammy Wynette. (O) Harper Valley PTA. (P) Buffalo Guns; The Gun and The Gravel; The Badge of Marshall Brennan. (Q) Dave 'Stringbean' Akeman. (R) Country Sunshine. (S) Dolly Parton. (T) Guitar. (U) Allen Reynolds. (V) Area Code 615. (W) Little Fauss and Big Halsy. (X) Fiddle. (Y) Eric Weissberg and Steve Mandel. (Z) Opryland Amusement Centre.

69 Starfile/The Carpenters

(A) Wes Jacobs. (B) The Hollywood Bowl Battle of the Bands. (C) RCA. (D) Spectrum. (E) Burt Bacharach. (F) Offering. (G) A US TV Bank commercial. (H) This Is Your Life. (I) Leon Russell and Bonnie Bramlett. (J) Now and Then.

70 Rock All-Sorts

(A) Neil Hefti. (B) Hello, Mom. (C) 1. Lee Hazlewood; 2. Frank Sinatra; 3. Lee Hazlewood. (D) On the movie soundtrack: A Man Could Get Killed. (E) Atco; Fontana. (F) The American Breed. (G) Coal Man. (H) The Cowsills. (I) Disraeli Gears. (J) Brown Eyed Girl. (K) The Mindbenders; Hotlegs; 10c.c. (L) Dublin, Ireland. (M) Jim Webb. (N) Matthew's Southern Comfort. (O) Willie The Pimp. (P) Sonny and Cher. (Q) Peter Asher. (R) Fool To Cry. (S) Johnny Mathis and Deniece Williams. (T) Roberta Joan Anderson. (U) Frankie Valli. (V) Duluth, Minnesota. (W) Flo and Eddie. (X) Gerry Beckley, Dewey Bunnell, Dan Peek, (Y) Abba. (Z) Friends.

71 Starfile/Pink Floyd

(A) 1965. (B) Syd Barrett, Rick Wright, Nick Mason, Roger Walters. (C) Pink Anderson and Floyd Council. (D) See Emily Play. (E) Dave Gilmour. (F) More. (G) Live At Pompeii. (H) Echoes. (I) Dark Side of the Moon. (J) Robert Wyatt.

72 All That Jazz

(A) Louis Armstrong. (B) Desafinado. (Slightly Out Of Tune). (C) Paul Desmond. (D) Stranger on the Shore; Leon Young String Chorale. (E) Julian 'Cannonball' and Nat. (F) 1958; Newport. (G) Django. (H) Ramsey Lewis, Red Holt, El Dee Young. (I) Play Misty for Me. (J) In Moscow. (K) Organ. (L) Booker T. Jones. (M) A-Tisket, A-Tasket; 1938. (N) Ruthann Friedman. (O) Comin' Home Baby. (P) Crystal. (Q) Charlie Parker. (R) April 4 1939. (S) Washington DC, April 29 1899. (T) Herb Ellis, Barney Kessel, Charlie Byrd. (U) Oscar Peterson, Ray Brown, Ed Thigpen. (V) Billie Holiday. (W) George Benson. (X) 1. Flute; 2. Violin; 3. Piano; 4. Tenor Sax; 5. Guitar; 6. Drums; 7. Vibes; 8. Bass; 9. Alto Sax; 10. Baritone Sax. (Y) Peggy Lee. (Z) CTI.

73 Starfile/Elton John

(A) Middlesex, England; March 25 1947. (B) Bluesology. (C) Dick James Music. (D) Empty Sky. (E) Born To Boogie. (F) Crocodile Rock. (G) Rocket Records. (H) Candle In The Wind. (I) Kiki Dee. (J) Song for Guy.

74 Rock All-Sorts

(A) The Detergents. (B) Fantasy. (C) Dory Previn. (D) Carol Kaye. (E) Donald Byrd. (F) Chi-Lites. (G) Betty Carter. (H) The Drifters. (I) Wayne Henderson. (J) A Lone Ranger. (K) It's My Party. (L) John Zacherle, (The Cool Ghoul). (M) Wonderful Summer. (N) The Shadows. (O) Happy Together. (P) Floyd Cramer. (Q) Yarrow, Stookey and Travers;Reunion. (R) Let's Dance ('62); The More I See You ('66). (S) Erik Darling, Lynne Taylor, Bill Svanoe. (T) Roger Miller. (U) Robert Parker. (V) Roxy Music. (W) The Pushbike Song. (X) Percy Faith. (Y) Seven. (Z) Ringo.

75 Disco Music

(A) Bernard Edwards and Nile Rodgers. (B) The Salsoul Orchestra. (C) Saturday. (D) Discobells. (E) I Make You Feel Like Dancin'. (F) Roy Ayers. (G) The Touch. (H) Barry, Robin and Maurice Gibb. (I) Stanley Turrentine. (J) Sylvester and Tip Wirrick.

76 Starfile/David Essex

(A) David Cook and The China Plates. (B) And The Tears Came Tumbling Down. (C) Mood Indigo. (D) Tommy Steele. (E) Assault. (F) 1971. (G) Jim MacLaine. (H) Jeff Wayne. (I) Gonna Make You A Star. (J) Evita.

77 The Crest of a Wave

(A) Lou Reed. (B) Egyptian. (C) Mink Deville. (D) The Buzzcocks. (E) The Clash. (F) The Electric Chairs. (G) Johnny Thunders. (H) My Aim Is True. (I) Ian Dury. (J) Edinburgh, Scotland. (K) Drummer Man. (L) The Voidoids. (M) My Boyfriend's Back. (N) Hey Joe. (O) Johnny Rotten, Steve Jones, Sid Vicious, Paul Cook. (P) Paul Weller. (Q) Ramones. (R) The Heartbreakers. (S) Rat Scabies. (T) Generation X. (U) Nick Lowe. (V) Shots From a Cold Nightmare. (W) Blondie. (X) Jonathan Richman. (Y) Iggy Pop. (Z) Tuff Darts, Mink Deville, The Shirts, Sun, Manster, The Laughing Dogs, Stuart's Hammer, The Miamis.

78 Starfile/Elvis Costello

(A) Flip City. (B) Declan MacManus, D. P. Costello. (C) 1977. (D) Steve Mason, Bruce Thomas, Peter Thomas. (E) My Aim Is True. (F) Nick Lowe. (G) Stiff; Radar. (H) Jazzmaster. (I) Radio, Radio. (J) Accidents Will Happen, Alison, Watching The Detectives.

79 Rock All-Sorts

(A) 1. From Russia With Love; 2. Goldfinger, Diamonds Are Forever; 3. Thunderball; 4. You Only Live Twice; 5. Live and Let Die; 6. Nobody Does It Better. (B) B. Bumble and The Stingers. (C) All Over The World. (D) Nine. (E) Pork Salad Annie. (F) Marshall, Hain. (G) Link Wray. (H) Arthur Alexander. (I) Traffic. (J) Lulu. (K) If I Had A Hammer. (L) Janice Johnson, Hazel Payne. (M) Kate Bush. (N) The Strangers. (O) Jim Jacobs and Warren Casey. (P) Edwin Hawkins Singers. (Q) Eric Clapton, Stevie Winwood, Rick Gretch, Ginger Baker. (R) The Newbeats. (S) Elvis Presley Fan Clubs. (T) Gilbert O'Sullivan. (U) Jackie Edwards. (V) Jimmy Webb. (W) Yes. (X) Brother Records. (Y) Duane and Gregg Allman. (Z) Randy Edelman.

Picture/Celluloid Answers

Picture Quiz 1

(A) Richard Carpenter and John Bettis. (B) The Carpenters, Karen Carpenter, Brother/Sister. (C) Calling Occupants of Interplanetary Craft (The Recognised Anthem of World Contact Day). (D) Disneyland.

Picture Quiz 2

(A) The Grand Ole Opry. (B) Country music. (C) Nashville, Tennessee.

Picture Quiz 3

(A) Phil Spector (standing), Gene Pitney (seated). (B) Now I've got a Witness (like Uncle Phil and Uncle Gene); The Rolling Stones. (C) Little By Little; Spector, Phelge. (D) Veronica 'Ronnie' Bennett.

Picture Quiz 4

(A) Bob Feldman; Jerry Goldstein; Richard Gottehrer. (B) The Strangeloves. (C) FGG. Productions. (D) The McCoys. (E) Sorrow. (F) Richard Gottehrer.

Picture Quiz 5

(A) Dick Dale. (B) 1. Surf Guitar. 2. Balboa. (C) The Del-Tones. (D) Let's Go Trippin'. (E) Beirut, Lebanon. (F) The First International Surfer's Stomp. (G) Surfer's Choice.

Picture Quiz 6

(A) Jet Harris. (B) Nivram. (C) April 16 1962. (D) Chills and Fever, May 11 1962. (E) Applejack; Tony Meehan. (F) Just For Fun.

Picture Quiz 7

(A) Tommy Sands, Nancy Sinatra. (B) Teenage. (C) Tony Rome. (D) Annette Funicello, The Parent Trap. (E) Speedway. (F) Love In A Goldfish Bowl.

Picture Quiz 8

(A) New York Dolls. (B) Johnny Thunders. (C) Jerry Nolan (second from left), Johnny Thunders (far right). (D) Johnny Thunders.

Celluloid Rock 1

(A) American Graffiti. (B) Paul Le Mat, Cindy Williams, Ronny Howard. (C) Flash Cadillac and The Continental Kids. (D) George Lucas (E) Wolfman Jack. (F) MCA.

Celluloid Rock 2

(A) Help. (B) Richard Lester. (C) Leo McKern. (D) July 29 1965. (E) Mal Evans. (F) Capitol.

Celluloid Rock 3

(A) The Man Who Fell To Earth. (B) Candy Clark, David Bowie. (C) Nicolas Roeg. (D) 1976.

Celluloid Rock 4

(A) Elvis Presley, Wendell Corey, Lizabeth Scott. (B) Loving You. (C) Hal Kanter. (D) 1957. (E) Deke Rivers. (F) RCA.

Celluloid Rock 5

(A) The Monkey's Uncle. (B) Annette Funicello, The Beach Boys. (C) 1964. (D) Robert Stevenson. (E) Buena Vista.

Celluloid Rock 6

(A) Rebel Without A Cause. (B) James Dean. (C) The Planetarium, Griffith Park, Southern California. (D) Plato. (E) Nicholas Ray. (F) Leonard Rosenman.

Celluloid Rock 7

(A) That'll Be The Day. (B) Claud Whatham. (C) David Essex (Jim MacLaine), Ringo Starr (Mike). (D) The 50's. (E) Keith Moon. (F) The Crickets.

Celluloid Rock 8

(A) Beach Party, Muscle Beach Party, Beach Blanket Bingo, Bikini Beach, How To Stuff A Wild Bikini. (B) William Asher. (C) 1963. (D) Frankie Avalon, Annette Funicello. (E) Malibu Beach.

Celluloid Rock 9

(A) Zabriske Point. (B) Michaelangelo Antonioni. (C) Mark Frechette, Daria Halprin. (D) 1969.

About the author

Rob Burt, the author, was born in Cardiff, Wales. He studied design and photography at Cardiff College of Art. On leaving, he became Art Editor of the BBC Radio One magazine *The Story of Pop.* Since then his activities include contributing numerous articles to popular music publications, selecting tracks for albums, designing sleeves and writing notes for them – among these are **Charlie Byrd's** *Byrd in the Hand,* **The Surfaris'** *Gone with the Wave,* and the soundtrack for the '78 Hot-Rod movie *Shut Down.*

ACKNOWLEDGEMENTS

The author and the publishers gratefully acknowledge the help of **Maureen O'Grady, David Wedgebury, Charles Webster, Brian Southall, Debbie Bennett, Dave Walters, Bob Fisher, Gordon Frewin, Graham Lauren, Steve Brendell, Peter Campbell, Todd Slaughter and The Official Elvis Presley Fan Club of Great Britain, Decca Records, EMI Records, Walt Disney Productions, Capitol Records, Columbia-EMI-Warner Film Distributors, Fantasy/Stax Records, Tamla Motown, London Weekend Television, Polydor and WEA.**

A special thanks to **Lizzie Burt.**